REVIEWS AND ENDORSEMENTS

For

Shaping Public Opinion:
How Real Advocacy Journalism™ Should Be Practiced

An appeal to contemporary journalists to utilize the model of Walter Lippmann.

"Too often in today's public discourse," argues Ellis, "the power and use of words seem to be ignored and disregarded" by pundits and others who are rewarded for hyperbole, partisanship, and ad hominem polemics. This book ... urges journalists to turn to the example of Pulitzer Prize–winning journalist Walter Lippmann.... A central argument is that Lippmann embodied what the author terms "Real Advocacy Journalism," which eschewed demagoguery and tribalism for a belief that "reason, logic, facts, truth, and clear and graphic language" were the "most effective instruments of public (mass) persuasion" as "society's elite as well as ordinary citizens looked to him for direction." Remarkably well-researched, the book uses Lippmann's published work and personal papers as well as original interviews with Lippmann's associates, from fellow journalists to his secretary.... Despite its sometimes-hagiographic treatment of Lippmann, the book admirably demonstrates the value of using the famed 20th-century journalist in 21st-century conversations about public knowledge, journalistic ethics, and public persuasion. In a world of tweets, sound bites, and hot takes, the eloquence, nuance, and logical style of Lippmann, as convincingly displayed by Ellis, is a welcome respite.

A...well-researched and convincingly argued case.

—Kirkus Reviews
The most trusted voice in book reviews since 1933

"Today's advocacy journalism slaps Americans in the face. 'It is partisan, biased, and blurs the lines between truth and lies, facts and fictions,' says award-winning author Janice Ellis. Ellis dives deep into the work of legendary Walter Lippmann, the original, authentic Real Advocacy Journalism™ newsman, and rigorously presents compelling, page-turning scholastic evidence of how true advocacy journalism can change the course of a nation."

—Donna Brazile
National Political Commentator, FOX, CNN
Syndicated Columnist
Author, and Adjunct Professor
Veteran Political Strategist

"The always thoughtful and insightful Janice Ellis, instead of simply complaining about the highly polarized nature of America's politics and its broader society today, proposes a rational and achievable solution: advocacy journalism rooted in the principles of fact-based reporting and careful analysis practiced so long and so well by the late Walter Lippmann. Her goal is not more strident voices yelling past each other but, rather, credible, wise journalism that helps our nation find its way in a post-fact world that's deeply anxious about the future. If you're a journalist, absorb this important book and then go practice what Ellis preaches."

—Bill Tammeus
Past president, National Society of Newspaper Columnists
Former Editorial Columnist, *The Kansas Star City*
Author of *Love, Loss and Endurance: A 9/11 Story of Resilience and Hope in an Age of Anxiety*

"As an advocate journalist for more than four decades, Dr. Ellis uses the power of words to address issues and forces—social, gender, racial, political, economic—that confront society today. In this powerful and timely treatise on how advocacy journalism affects public opinion and the political arena, she draws from the principles and practices of her mentor, the venerable Walter Lippman as she implores contemporary advocate journalists to seriously consider his valuable lessons and stay committed to what she calls *Real Advocacy Journalism* to achieve the greater good for society. Essential reading for today."

—Chanticleer Reviews
Discovering Today's Best Books through
Editorial Book Reviews

"Grounded in Walter Lippman's concepts of how the media should function in a democracy, Janice Ellis reiterates his principles and practices in her latest book, *Shaping Public Opinion: How Real Advocacy Journalism™ Should Be Practiced*. In the text, she skillfully juxtaposes the intersectionality of the purveyance of information by biased pundits and conspiracy theorists with advocacy journalists like herself who have undertaken the responsibility to "wake-up" the consumer with transparent truths. Ellis seeks to bridge the gap between the preponderance of conflicting conspiracy theories interwoven in the media with truth, which mesmerize and confuse people into accepting information that interferes with their ability to question, examine, and respond to alternate points of view needed to form a solid foundation for making personal choices about what to accept and what to reject when thinking critically about academic, social, and political issues that impact their lives."

—Lillie Smith Bailey, PhD
Associate Professor of English (Retired)
Author of *The Point of It All*

"Finally, a book with practical solutions to help journalists go beyond superficial reporting of angry claims and counter-claims from political opponents."

—Cynthia Newsome
Veteran Television Anchor
KSHB, Kansas City

"In determining the winner of the Grand Prize for the Nellie Bly Nonfiction Journalism Award, Chanticleer International Book Awards judges seek the best journalistic works in social science, data-driven reports, equality and justice, ethics, human rights, activist groups, crimes and corruption, environmental, whistle-blowers, health and medicine, and politics. Among many great finalists, *Shaping Public Opinion: How Real Advocacy Journalism™ Should Be Practiced* was the 2019 grand prize winner. The award was announced at the Chanticleer International Authors Conference in September 2020."

—Chanticleer International Book Awards

Shaping Public Opinion

How Real Advocacy Journalism™ Should Be Practiced

Janice S. Ellis, PhD

SHAPING PUBLIC OPINION
How Real Advocacy Journalism™ Should Be Practiced
By Janice S. Ellis, PhD
1. POL04600 2. POL043000 3. POL065000
PAPERBACK: 978-1-949642-66-7
HARD COVER: 978-1-949642-67-4
EBOOK: 978-1-949642-68-1
Library of Congress Control Number: 2021906171

Cover design by LEWIS AGRELL

Printed in the United States of America

Authority Publishing
11230 Gold Express Dr. #310-413
Gold River, CA 95670
800-877-1097
www.AuthorityPublishing.com

To those active and aspiring journalists, political columnists/commentators, pundits, and politicians who work, and want to work, to influence publics in building a better society.

To the publics that are being influenced by them.

To those who study, teach, and are concerned about the displacement of Real Advocacy Journalism™, and who are willing to play their role in restoring it for the betterment of society.

TABLE OF CONTENTS

PREFACE

The power and use of words still matter in contemporary society, perhaps more so than ever. Words have mattered since the dawn of civilization. But too often in today's public discourse, especially when it comes to politics and governing, the power and use of words seem to be ignored and disregarded. This is evident with the myriad of political commentators in print, radio, television, and online media attempting to analyze public policy, political persons, and events—rationally or irrationally. What better time than now to revisit how one of the most renowned and influential political columnists of the twentieth century perceived and practiced, what I describe in this book as *Real Advocacy Journalism*™. Walter Lippmann in his role as a political columnist, an advocate journalist, provides the theoretical principles and practical application of *Real Advocacy Journalism*™, which is so needed today in shaping public opinion and public policy.

The potential power and effective use of words to change the course of a nation were reaffirmed during my graduate study at the University of Wisconsin. In one of my political science classes, I had as assigned reading two of Lippmann's books, *A Preface to Politics* and *Essays in the Public Philosophy*. I stumbled upon a third book, *Public Opinion*. In addition to those three books, Lippmann wrote a number of seminal books on the theory and philosophy of politics and government, and the role of the public in fostering the good society.

Also, Lippmann penned a column for nearly forty years that was syndicated in more than two hundred and fifty newspapers across the United States and in newspapers in twenty-five other countries. In his newspaper columns, he clarified issues, influenced and nudged American presidents, world leaders, and ordinary citizens to advance public policy decisions that would secure the greatest good for the greatest number of people.

Walter Lippmann wrote his books and columns during major periods of calm and anxiety, during wars and economic crises as America was continuing to find her footing as an emerging nation and her place on the world stage.

The major research for this book was conducted as I completed my doctoral thesis for the PhD in Communication Arts at the University of Wisconsin, and from additional research I have completed since. Through a grant from the Graduate School of the University, I was able to conduct research at the Sterling Library at Yale University, New Haven, Connecticut, where I had access to the Robert O. Anthony Collection of Walter Lippmann's published works, and to the Lippmann Papers. The Robert O. Anthony Collection consists, without exception, of all known materials written by Lippmann during all phases of his career, as well as a comprehensive collection of articles written about him. The Walter Lippmann papers consist of his personal papers, letters, and handwritten articles and manuscripts of his writings. I also used the materials available in the Library of the Wisconsin State Historical Society and the Memorial Library at the University of Wisconsin.

Probably no other journalist, and practitioner of *Real Advocacy Journalism*™, has had a career so carefully and completely documented.

I lived and breathed the works of Lippmann as I completed my doctoral thesis. I was captivated by his views of the role of public opinion in shaping public policy, and the importance of the political columnist/commentator, the politician/political leader, to be men and women of "light and leading."

I was fortunate to be granted interviews with three of Lippmann's contemporaries: Eric Sevareid, author, journalist, international correspondent, and commentator on the *CBS Evening News with Walter Cronkite*; James Reston, author, journalist, and columnist for *The New York Times*; and Marquis Childs, author, journalist, and columnist for the *St. Louis Post-Dispatch*.

Also, I was able to interview Elizabeth Farmer Midgley, Lippmann's personal secretary and assistant for the last ten years of his writing career. During the time of our interview, Ms. Midgley was producer of *CBS Weekend News*.

These interviews were invaluable in providing further insight into Walter Lippmann, the man, and how he perceived his role as a journalist, political columnist, as a persuader of publics. Portions of those interviews are published for the first time in this book.

As Karl E. Meyer of *The New York Times* editorial staff wrote in "The Editorial Notebook," back on October 23, 1980, several years following Lippmann's death: "It was the brilliance of Lippmann's work—his public face—that made him a legend for a half a century."

Decades have passed since Walter Lippmann wrote his final "Today and Tomorrow" newspaper column. And to many journalists, pundits, and politicians who have since entered the public and political arena, Lippmann's awesome reputation may well be unknown, something of a mystery, or much of his brilliant writing has been forgotten. Lippmann once said a political writer is "just a puzzled man making notes...drawing sketches in the sand which the sea will wash away."

It is hoped that this book will introduce, re-introduce, or serve as a reminder of just how meaningful Lippmann's sketches were, how much they shed light, back then, and how they can illumine a path for us to rise above the political messaging morass in which we find ourselves today. The book shows how Lippmann's writings defined and set the standard for a form of public discourse, which I call *Real Advocacy Journalism*™.

More importantly, *Shaping Public Opinion: How Real Advocacy Journalism*™ *Should Be Practiced* will show how the tenets and applications of *Real Advocacy Journalism*™, punditry at its best, which have been extracted from Lippmann's theories and practices, are sorely needed today amid the cacophony of voices that seek to create and shape public perceptions, opinions, and actions—many of whom adhering to no standard other than their own. There is so much advocacy in all areas of public dialogue by special interest groups, zealots, and extremists. It is becoming more prevalent and acceptable, if not commonplace, as a primary news source for many people in contemporary society. It is being done under the guise of *Real Advocacy Journalism*™. Unfortunately, however, much of it fails to meet the noble purpose or required elements of *Real Advocacy Journalism*™.

Shaping Public Opinion will have special resonance with journalists, political columnists/commentators, pundits, political leaders, other influencers of public opinion, the professors who teach and the students who study them as well as citizens who are concerned about the trajectory and course of our national and international political dialogue.

There is a growing, if not urgent, need to understand the difference between the advocacy journalism being practiced today and *Real Advocacy Journalism*™; and, more importantly, to readily recognize when one or the other is at play in trying to influence public opinion, or urge a call to action.

INTRODUCTION

What is the difference between advocacy journalism as it is practiced today and *Real Advocacy Journalism*™ that is described and advanced in this book?

Much of the advocacy journalism practiced today is partisan, biased, and often blurs the lines between truth and lies, facts and fiction, and often presents fake news as real news. The purpose and objectives of such advocacy journalism constitute propaganda to gain public support for the interest and agenda of a few, a special interest group, or a small constituency rather than for the good of the majority.

Advocacy journalism across different media has become a pernicious tool often carried out by partisans, zealots, and extremists, pushing separatist ideologies rather than unity, without any mention or consideration for objectivity or transparency. This is evident in print media with publications focused solely on targeted agendas such as conservative, liberal, the far right, the far left. It is also evident in electronic media with cable stations and programs whose content is designed to present and support only one side of the political spectrum, covering only one type of incidents or stories that occur rather than presenting all sides of the political spectrum, and covering a variety of incidents and stories. There is often little or no effort to present the complete picture.

These practices have given rise to the idea, the notion, even concern about whether there is systemic media bias that pervades contemporary public communication and discourse.

Complex local, regional, national, and global issues are often covered and treated with a biased and simplistic categorization. This happens all too frequently when the public is asked to form an opinion or support an action. Historically, and currently, this occurs in issue areas such as: should we go to war or support a war; what is the appropriate health care policy for the majority of citizens; how can gun violence be curbed; what are the distinctions between terrorism carried out by a foreign enemy, naturalized citizen, or a naturally-born citizen; is climate change a real threat to civilization or a man-made hoax; is the Covid-19 pandemic a massive conspiracy; and, on and on....

A constant barrage of simplistic, distorted, biased, untruthful, non-factual treatments can only be a disservice to a dependent, hopeful, ill-informed, trusting public.

What passes as legitimate advocacy journalism is often characterized by rumors, inuendo, conspiracy theories, sensationalism, and all kinds of drama that is carried out in mainstream media, social media, and most critically in conversations, presentations, and public forums—within whatever orbit of influence of the practitioner—all reinforcing false information that leads to further divisiveness, poor policy decisions, detrimental actions, and sometimes apathy with no actions at all when they are critically needed.

Today, advocacy journalism has taken a radical turn from how *Real Advocacy Journalism*™ should be practiced. Imagine how better off society would be if *Real Advocacy Journalism*™ was understood, embraced, and practiced. Our hope is that this book will help change the tide.

Shaping Public Opinion: How Real Advocacy Journalism™ *Should Be Practiced* is a critical examination of the theory, principles, and practices of one of the foremost and influential political columnists of the last one hundred years. The book identifies the situations in contemporary society, which Walter Lippmann perceived as exigencies compelling the creation of a genre of advocatory discourse, *Real Advocacy Journalism*™, to assist in the management of public affairs. The book also shows how Lippmann defined and codified the genre as an honorable and needed profession in contemporary society.

Evidence is provided, which shows Lippmann was a model practitioner back when advocacy journalism, in any form, was not a part of the common lexicon and was considered an anathema to objective unbiased journalistic standards, or an oxymoron at best. Emphasis is placed on the growing importance of establishing and maintaining the rules of engagement, today, for practitioners of *Real Advocacy Journalism*™ as more and more people rely on it as their primary source of news from websites, social media, talk radio, cable TV, blogs, and as reliance on traditional newspapers continues to decline.

Through his newspaper column, Walter Lippmann influenced presidents, kings, and all manner of powerful leaders. Society's elite as well as ordinary citizens looked to him for direction, for a perspective on what was happening in government, politics, the economy, in national and world affairs. Lippmann was awarded a special Pulitzer Prize for journalism as a national syndicated columnist. The citation states that the prize was bestowed for "the wisdom, perception and high sense of responsibility with which he has commented for many years on national and international affairs."

Walter Lippmann also wrote seminal books about politics, morals, public opinion, and what constitutes the good society.

How was Walter Lippmann able to be so influential, so persuasive in shaping public opinion, and in many cases public policy? How was he able to engage such a vast and varied audience for such a long period of time? What was his communication style, his methods and techniques of public persuasion? These questions compel contemporary advocate journalists, pundits, politicians, other influencers of public opinion, the students that study them, as well as followers and other observers, to examine the works of Walter Lippmann.

This revisit into the life and writings of Lippmann is to cull out and focus specifically on his theory and practice of *Real Advocacy Journalism*™, which seems too often to elude contemporary public media, and to offer an evaluation of him as the pragmatic and model practitioner. The methods of *Real Advocacy Journalism*™ practiced and recommended by Lippmann in functioning as an advocate journalist, a political columnist, a pundit, a persuader of publics, are very valuable and offer instructive guideposts for today's practitioners.

To carve out Lippmann's theory of *Real Advocacy Journalism*™, the principles and practices it contains, one must consult his books, as well as his newspaper columns. Lippmann functioned throughout his literary career in two media—one of books where he developed his theories of politics, morals, the public philosophy, and public opinion; and the other of short essays, i.e., his columns, where he applied and tested those theories. The contents of his works in both realms are the focus of this book.

Shaping Public Opinion presents a powerful and compelling case of why the writings of Lippmann have so much meaning and resonance for twenty-first century journalists, pundits, politicians, and the publics they reach. *Shaping Public Opinion* shows how these roles carry so much weight and responsibility in shaping the perceptions and opinions of a public that is constantly bombarded by competing, complex, and often false or distorted communication messages, passing as *Real Advocacy Journalism*™. Members of this same public are pursued and required to lend their voices and support for the adoption and execution of important public policies and practices.

The first four chapters establish Walter Lippmann as the father of *Real Advocacy Journalism*™. The last four chapters show how Lippmann carved out and practiced the premises and elements of *Real Advocacy Journalism*™. Guiding principles and requirements are presented for current and aspiring advocate journalists, political columnists/commentators, pundits, politicians, and other persuaders of publics to consider and put into action; and how a current advocate journalist puts these principles into practice.

Chapter One, Who Was Walter Lippmann, summarizes Lippmann's career as an advocate journalist, the fundamental beliefs and principles that guided his writings, and the vast national and international audience that paid attention to him.

Chapter Two, Lippmann the Political Columnist: A Real Advocate Journalist Emerges, examines Lippmann as dean of American political columnists, as the mentor and trendsetter for the political columnists of the twentieth century, which he was regarded by many of his contemporaries and those who sought to analyze and study him.

Chapter Three, Lippmann Evaluated as a Real Advocate Journalist, provides a brief survey of the critical appraisals of Lippmann's career as a political columnist, an advocate journalist, from his contemporaries, providing insight into why his voice, analysis, and punditry were so highly regarded. Included are excerpts from the author's unpublished interviews with Eric Sevareid, career journalist and commentator on the *CBS Evening News with Walter Cronkite*; James Reston, long-standing journalist, political columnist for *The New York Times*; and Marquis Childs, noted journalist and political columnist of the *St. Louis Post-Dispatch*.

Chapter Four, The Need, Role, and Function of *Real Advocacy Journalism*™, examines the situations in contemporary society, which Lippmann perceived as conditions compelling the need for the genre of discourse, *Real Advocacy Journalism*™, to assist in the management of public affairs. Such conditions include: a) man's inability, because of the complexity of society, to make spontaneous policy decisions as a collective; b) the weaknesses in the public communication system, and the channels and methods of information flow, which often convey inadequate and incomplete information and therefore impede responsible decision; and c) the urgent need to promulgate advocatory dialogue in determining the right course of action.

Chapter Five, Samples of *Real Advocacy Journalism*™ Applied to Persistent Issues, identifies and describes the advocatory techniques Lippmann practiced. More importantly, it confirms the weightiness and responsibility with which he perceived his role to be that of a reliable source of truth, enlightenment, and leadership—critical elements that should govern the work of an influencer of publics. This chapter provides examples of good, effective, and responsible *Real Advocacy Journalism*™ at work as Lippmann addresses three issues he thinks are critical to the long-term well-being of a society: 1) the role of government; 2) the role of the public; and 3) the role of the public philosophy. The chapters profile and provide compelling evidence of Lippmann's advocatory techniques and communication style, which become clear when one focuses on his treatment of these inherent conditions in contemporary society—conditions he dealt with in both his books and newspaper columns. These chapters specifically deal with how his newspaper columns were created since they reached a large and changing audience. The columns are examined for form, structure, advocatory techniques, and literary style in order to delineate requisite characteristics and requirements of the genre of *Real Advocacy Journalism*™ in its best and most effective form, which are instructive for today's practitioners.

Chapter Six, What *Real Advocacy Journalism*™ Requires of the Practitioner, describes the abilities, characteristics, focus, and skill sets necessary to carry out and achieve the purposes of *Real Advocacy Journalism*™.

Chapter Seven, *Real Advocacy Journalism*™ in the Twenty-First Century: Rules of Engagement, summarizes what seminal and lasting contributions Lippmann made to a contemporary theory of *Real Advocacy Journalism*™, the tenets and application of which are sorely needed and should be practiced by those who seek to create and shape public perceptions, opinions, and actions. These tenets are so critical today during a time when trust in government as the protector of the public's best interest, and the media as the impartial watchdog, continue to erode. The correct practice of *Real Advocacy Journalism*™ should be better understood and promulgated. Critical prerequisites and guiding principles in carrying out the weighty responsibility of being an influencer of publics are offered to future advocate journalists, pundits, and politicians for consideration as they ponder entering or being a part of such needed and noble professions.

Chapter Eight, Impact of Lippmann on An Advocate Journalist: A Personal Account, describes how Lippmann's theory and practice impacted the author in her work as a newspaper columnist, radio commentator, and online commentator.

This book is a call to action for persuaders of publics to practice *Real Advocacy Journalism*™ to preserve and advance a better society, rather than the degraded form that is becoming pervasive across all media.

1

WHO WAS WALTER LIPPMANN?

Walter Lippmann functioned throughout his adult life in the maze of politics, governance, and trying to determine the role of the public in fostering what is in its best interest at any given time, particularly at those crossroads that could determine the course of entire countries or human history. What role did Lippmann play as guardian of the public interest? What contributions did he make in helping the practitioners of public persuasion—journalists, pundits, and politicians—lead and direct the masses?

For nearly a half-century, through books and a syndicated newspaper column, three generations were "led through the maze of political affairs"[1] by Lippmann's concern, his vision, his analysis. He felt a moral obligation to be a man of light and leading. He wrote in *A Preface to Morals* that "one function of the moralist is not to exhort men to be good but to elucidate what the good is."[2] And if the moralist "is to be listened to, and if he is to deserve a hearing among his fellows, he must set himself this task which is so much humbler than to command and so much more difficult than to exhort: he must seek to anticipate and to supplement the insight of his fellow men into the problems of their adjustment to reality. He must find ways to make clear and ordered and expressive those concerns which are latent but overlaid and confused by their preoccupations and misunderstandings."[3]

Fundamentally, Lippmann believed that issues and politics matter and how they are regarded and treated are paramount in determining the best course of action. Reasoned discourse is at the core. He held the conviction that men can live a life of reason, that they can achieve understanding and direction through the process of reasoning. And he was committed to the process of reasoning and felt that those with a special gift for analysis and understanding of issues and problems had a responsibility to do what they can to illuminate the path for others. "The hallmark of responsible comment is not to sit in judgment on events as an idle spectator, but to enter imaginatively into the role of a participant in the action," he wrote in tribute to a renowned newspaper editor. "Responsibility consists in sharing the burden of men, directing what is to be done, or the burden of offering some other course of action in the mood of one who has realized what it would mean to undertake it."[4]

Walter Lippmann assumed that responsibility and spent his life deliberating about what was the good or best end for contemporary man to pursue in fostering the good society.

During the early years of the twentieth century to the time of his death in 1974, Lippmann wrote on subjects of public concern in a number of books,[5] hundreds of magazine articles,[6] and thousands of newspaper columns.[7] His abiding theme was the precepts and practices of liberal democracy in the Western World—both the transitory and enduring. He wrestled tenaciously with the old tensions of liberal democracy: liberty versus authority, populism versus constitutionalism, the rule of the majority versus the rights of the minority.[8] He was equally concerned with the newer tensions: individualism and collectivism, the private sector and the public sector, the ruling elite, and the dormant masses, and what he called periods of "drift" and "mastery."[9] Some versions of these same issues still occupy public discourse today.

Lippmann also responded to the many political and social issues of the hour back then, similar to many of those we face today, both domestic and foreign. He dealt with the issues of war and peace as America was confronted with them, the problems of an unstable and deteriorating economy, the state of political education, foreign policy. He evaluated the efficacy of governmental programs, political leadership, policy decisions on the part of elected officials, the role of an unlearned, uninformed public in policymaking, the shortcomings, and impending dangers of mass communication, the imperative upon contemporary society to redefine the concept of private property, and the concept of majority rule, and the imperative upon contemporary society to recommit itself to what he calls the public philosophy, the tradition of civility.

But aside from the vastness in scope of subject matter and the quantity of his work, Lippmann was considered by many of his contemporaries as the most profound American political thinker in the twentieth century.[10] As a political theorist on the one hand and a newspaper columnist on the other, Lippmann spent over a half-century analyzing and theorizing about the social and political environment in which he lived. Even though he appeared to be immersed in day-to-day governmental conflicts and issues, he had an acute, longstanding concern about the nature of man, the role of government in a democratic society, and what should be the relationship of one to the other.

Who was Lippmann's audience? Unlike many of the major columnists/commentators today, Lippmann addressed a large, diverse audience. At the time, Lippmann's audience was the largest ever to pay thoughtful attention to a serious American writer.[11] Unlike many philosophers and theorists, Lippmann spent most of his life performing analysis and criticism "not in philosophic tracts for few, but in newspapers and periodicals which reached a wide audience."[12] Furthermore, he did it, first in a period of "national contraction" during the twenties, and second, in a period of "revolutionary expansion" of American influence, when old habits of thought and political action were in the process of change in countries across the world.[13]

This expansion of influence in America and abroad lasted for decades, most notably following World War II and until the latter part of the twentieth century. America's continual influence in the twenty-first century is yet to be determined, and certainly in question in the current national and international climate.

During its height of popularity, Lippmann's column was syndicated in more than two hundred and fifty newspapers in the United States and in newspapers in twenty-five foreign countries. In London it was published in the *Daily Mail*, in Tokyo in the *Yomiuri Shimbun*, in Paris in *Le Figaro* as well as the *Herald Tribune* European edition. His column was published in such faraway lands as Greece, Belgium, Australia, Spain, India, Brazil, New Zealand, Uruguay, and Sweden.[14]

To better understand the theoretical premises that underlie Lippmann's case for and the practice of *Real Advocacy Journalism*™, we must consult several of his seminal books. They include: *Public Opinion*, *The Phantom Public*, *The Good Society*, *A Preface to Morals*, and *Essays in the Public Philosophy*.[15] It is within these books that Lippmann addresses in detail, and repeatedly, the theoretical underpinnings of the three major issues that seem to consume him during his career. They are: 1) What should be the role of government; 2) What is the role of the public in determining public policy; and 3) What is the role of the public philosophy in fostering the good society.

To better understand how Lippmann practiced *Real Advocacy Journalism*™, his newspaper columns written for nearly four decades under the banner, "Today and Tomorrow," are examined for the advocatory techniques exemplified in them.

During the period between 1931 and 1967, Lippmann wrote over four thousand columns.[16] The series appeared in its original form in the *New York Herald Tribune* from 1931 to 1962 and in *The Washington Post* from 1963 to 1967. The *Herald Tribune* and *Washington Post* regularly published Lippmann's column with the standard heading and topical sub-heading Lippmann provided in these papers, the column appeared in a fixed position on the page. Many of the other papers in which the column appeared varied this procedure, supplying their own titles and deleting or omitting portions of the column pretty much at will.[17]

The three areas identified above that Lippmann dealt with repeatedly in his books and columns have been selected for in-depth analysis and illustrative purposes. Examining these issues demonstrate how Lippmann dealt with the same subjects in two different media—books and shorter essays. They also demonstrate how Lippmann tried to disseminate basic ideas, basic philosophical concerns, and particular solutions for those concerns, to a larger, more diverse audience. His use of knowledge, facts, reason, and other techniques become evident—all of which are so critical to the practice of *Real Advocacy Journalism*™ that is both ethical and honorable.

2

LIPPMANN THE POLITICAL COLUMNIST: A REAL ADVOCATE JOURNALIST EMERGES

According to Robert O. Anthony, the curator of Lippmann's work, "the secret of his ability to carry his vigorous opinions into widely different newspapers lay in his *expert information, his reasonableness of temper, his complete honesty and his profound attachment to the principles of liberty*." (Emphasis added.) Anthony further states, that "his independence was unquestioned perhaps because, as someone put it, 'he addressed himself to possibilities, not imagings.'"[1]

Addressing himself to possibilities, to ends which could be attainable, set Lippmann apart, made his readers take him seriously and made them look to him for vision and enlightenment. With the "Today and Tomorrow" column, he became more concerned, as the title of the column suggests, with broader issues which had far-reaching implications for a larger number of people (often society generally), for a longer period of time.

"Today and Tomorrow" gained popularity rapidly. In less than two years, syndication had grown from twelve papers to one hundred and twelve in 1933. Lippmann was speaking "directly to the readers of many of the most important journals in two-thirds of all the states in the Union. He had the largest public daily of any publicist in the world."[2]

Lippmann's career as "dean of the columnists" had begun.[3] He not only had far-reaching influence in the shaping of American opinion and public policy, he almost single-handedly "raised the standards of journalistic commentary in this country."[4] As testimony to the universality of that opinion, Henry Allen writing an article in 1980 about Lippmann in *The Washington Post* declared that "Walter Lippmann wrote some of the greatest political analysis columns in history. *He invented the form*, back in 1931."[5] (Emphasis added.) Marquis Childs observes, "The Lippmann column syndicated in newspapers throughout the country was a *model of lucidity, clarity and penetrating comment* on the flow of events."[6] (Emphasis added.)

Commentators who followed Lippmann were profoundly influenced by the content and style of his writing. Ronald Steel, Lippmann's biographer, says: "I don't know that anybody could do what Lippmann did again."[7] And Thomas Griffith, writing an article in *Time* magazine states, "Calling Walter Lippmann the last of the great political columnists is an implied rebuke to his successors, suggesting that they don't make them like that anymore. Well, they don't. A man not afraid to be caught reasoning in print, Lippmann intellectually dominated the editorial pages of American newspapers for a half-century.... Wrong he might sometimes be, but rarely uncertain."[8]

Even though Lippmann ceased writing as a political columnist in 1967 and died in 1974, in 1980, more than a decade after his columns no longer appeared, they were characterized and hailed as the prototype of what political commentary, i.e., *Real Advocacy Journalism*™ should be about—what the focus and purpose should be. Lippmann's contemporaries as well as others, subsequently, who were interested in his work came to see that his form of public commentary set an unprecedented standard. While they did not label it, it is clear that Lippmann set the standard and practiced, as it should be, what now can be defined as *Real Advocacy Journalism*™.

Lippmann's study and unwavering concerns about the public's best interests are real clues to the preparation required to practice *Real Advocacy Journalism*™.

First, Lippmann had a thirst for knowledge. He wanted to not only understand the workings of government, public policies, human nature, and what makes for a vibrant and healthy society, he wanted to explore how to make the weaknesses stronger, how to turn challenges and obstacles into opportunities for sustainment and growth. In gaining that understanding, he studied and interacted with the best experts and best minds available to him. He wanted to be on sound footing, he wanted to put forth the best advice as he addressed his attentive publics on whatever issue or topic that was before them. He learned, respected, and appreciated the value of vigorous debate, discussion, and reason when confronted with difficult and conflicting circumstances. This appreciation took deep roots during his years at Harvard, continued, and blossomed throughout his career.

Secondly, Lippmann, before he became a nationally syndicated political columnist, had first-hand experience in the affairs of government, working in different capacities for US presidents and their administrations. In those capacities, he was engaged in national and international issues and affairs. He immersed himself, studied them, researched, and compiled papers and documents offering short- and long-term solutions for the issues or crisis being dealt with at the time. He, no doubt, gained an abiding appreciation for the difficulty in arriving at solutions that putting in place public policies that were good for a nation and the majority of its citizenry.

Thirdly, Lippmann learned, and put into practice very early, the value of accurate and effective communication, particularly as a journalist first and subsequently as a political columnist. His writing career as a persuader of publics began with the first article he wrote for his high school newspaper. Writing with compelling clarity, fluidity, and factual accuracy continued during his days at Harvard, during his various positions with some of the major newspapers upon leaving Harvard, and in the following decades with his syndicated column.

Preparation, respect for facts, truth, objectivity, and an overriding concern to identify and to foster those ends that lead to a better society are paramount in the practice of *Real Advocacy Journalism*™.

3

LIPPMANN EVALUATED AS A REAL ADVOCATE JOURNALIST

Observations and critical assessments throughout Walter Lippmann's career as a political columnist reveal that he was highly regarded.

The death of Lippmann on December 14, 1974 at age eighty-five ended a distinguished career, and the reviews which followed were testimony to how he was perceived and regarded. Louis Lyons, in an article about Lippmann, declared over a Boston's public television station that Lippmann was "the lodestar for the noblest journalists of his time, the first political columnist in the modern sense, and he had no peer."[1]

At Lippmann's memorial service in Washington, friends, editors, publishers, journalists, and governmental officials spoke of what Lippmann had meant to twentieth-century America. Senator J. William Fulbright, representing Arkansas from January 1945 until December 1974 and the longest serving chairman in history of the Senate Foreign Relations Committee, said he regarded Lippmann as the man who tried to make sense out of "an incomprehensible and irrational world," and whose career was devoted to "enlightening and civilizing his fellow Americans."

Fellow journalists spoke of Lippmann's role in instructing younger writers. Phillip Geyelin, editor of *The Washington Post* said: "He taught us how to think and what to think about. He was a philosopher with a deadline." Author Schlesinger, Jr., former adviser to President Kennedy, said Lippmann's own test of a great leader would be determined by whether the leader's survivors would carry on his work. Applying this standard, Schlesinger regarded Lippmann as an eminent success in that his standards of objectivity and his judicious perspectives still impress and instruct. Lippmann's conviction was that the good journalist strays away from the calcified centers of power and becomes, as Schlesinger pointed out, "an educator in public policy."[2]

Writers and major print media stopped to pay tribute to Walter Lippmann. Ronald Steel in the process of writing Lippmann's biography reflected:

> Because he helped elucidate the obscure, because he stood for principle in a climate of expediency, because he reminded us that there are values that transcend momentary obsessions, because he believed in the light of reason, and the ability of man to master his own weakness, because he was a humanist whose life exemplified the stoicism he raised, we shall all be poorer for living in a world where the voice of Walter Lippmann is stilled.[3]

Joseph Kraft writing in *The Washington Post* characterizes Lippmann's role in twentieth-century America. He says:

> The essential Lippmann was intellectually responsible. He worked hard to make out what he really thought. He tried to examine the unforeseen bad consequences of pure intentions. He searched his mind for breaks and continuities, the recurrent pattern of affairs, the

morphology of politics and diplomacy. "Today and Tomorrow," as he called his column, set the bewildering variety of daily events in the context of the long past and the big maps. Lippmann explained why things happened and more important why they didn't happen. Even when Lippmann was wrong, he was illuminating. His influence came out from rubbing shoulders with celebrities. It flowed from the independence of his thought, the penetration of his analysis.[4]

Elizabeth Peer, writing for *Newsweek* says: "For nearly four decades, Walter Lippmann's thoughtful and erudite columns on world affairs were required reading for millions of Americans." Peer observes that "Walter Lippmann perfected a rare ability to impose verbal order on chaos... American journalism lost one of its calmest, clearest voices of reason. The controlled lucidity of his prose, the independence of his judgments, the austere assumption that his readers turned to him for logic and enlightenment rather than entertainment or scoops earned Lippmann two Pulitzer Prizes and a reputation of mythic proportions."[5]

Time magazine dealt with how Lippmann maintained a cool level head during times of crises and put forth reasoned responses: "Crises...did not panic him. In a speech forty years ago, he said: 'The world will go on somehow, and more crises, will follow. It will go on best, however, if among us there are men who have stood apart, who refused to be anxious or too much concerned, who were cool and inquiring, and had their eyes on a longer past and a longer future.' He was such a man to the end!"[6]

Harrison Salisbury, writing for *New Times* proclaimed: "It was Lippmann's gift [and it was a talent which became keener with the years] to cut through the murk of public debate and expose the true heart of the matter with extraordinary clarity.

He made the complex clear. He had a sense for the jugular of issues...."[7]

The tributes given to Lippmann did not overlook his weakness and flaws. In *Newsweek*, Peer points out that sometimes Lippmann's judgments were questionable. "He seemed to underestimate Roosevelt and overestimate Wendell Willkie, and he dismissed Barry Goldwater as politically inconsequential prior to the Arizonian's blitz of the GOP in 1964."[8] *Time* observes that Lippmann's "refusal to interpret events according to doctrine struck some critics as vacillation. But, in fact, Lippmann shifted far less than did the political spectrum against which his position was measured." A more serious weakness exhibited by Lippmann, according to *Time*, was his "detachment from the mire of human affairs. Comfortable in the company of statesmen and scholars, he did not always comprehend popular emotions or their impact on public policy." As an example, *Time* cites how Lippmann discussed the Cold War, "arguing reasonably that the Soviet Union and China would inevitably dominate their 'orbits' as the United States did its own. This view is now grudgingly echoed in US foreign policy, but Lippmann's refusal to give weight to the explosive emotions of the Cold War drew much criticism when tensions were at their peak."[9]

The more serious criticisms of Lippmann, the man, came in the aftermath of the Steel biography. *Newsweek's* Peter Prescott, sums it up accordingly:

> Lippmann was no stranger to error. He mistook the reforms of the New Deal for revolution and once excused Hitler as "the authentic voice of a genuinely civilized people." Throughout his life he defended the wartime internment of Japanese Americans. Far more dismaying, because a voice as authoritative as his might have made a difference, was Lippmann's distaste for his fellow Jews.

An assimilationist, raised to think of Jewishness as an infirmity to be ignored, he rejected "tribal loyalty" and criticized the rich and vulgar and pretentious Jews for being "conspicuous." I do not regard Jews as innocent victims, he once wrote. At no time, during World War II or after, did he write of the horrors inflicted on Jews, nor did he urge America to welcome Jewish refugees.[10]

Ronald Steel speaks of Lippmann's "intellectual flexibility," his "evenhandedness" that irritated political partisans, and his mistake in not dealing with a few key issues or dealing with them inadequately. But after years of studying Lippmann, Steel concludes: "When he went wrong, it was in trying to impose an intellectual grid...on situations about which he had conflicting feelings... He felt an insider's responsibility for making the system work." Throughout his career, "he was never alienated and was in no sense a radical."[11]

This observation that Lippmann's works are in response to, and a reflection of the times has significant implications in terms of the role of the political columnist and *Real Advocacy Journalism*™ as a genre of discourse, which are instructive for practitioners today.

In matters of specific controversy, one can find significant differences in Lippmann's positions over the years. The central issue is not whether Lippmann is more of a pragmatist, and idealist, or humanist, or whether he successfully integrated aspects of each of these doctrines into a unique philosophical doctrine of his own or has failed to do so. Rather, the issue is how and on what basis did he choose to apply these philosophical systems to public problems as they arose—adhering to a theory or theories he believed accurate and applicable, and advocating courses of action reasoned to be expedient and profitable or, with equal conviction and swiftness, abandoning a theory he found invalid, and retreating from a course of action he perceived as inappropriate and detrimental.

More importantly, what should be noted is that what appears to be inconsistency of thought is in reality characteristic of the genre of discourse in which Lippmann was engaged, *Real Advocacy Journalism*™. It is indicative of Lippmann adjusting to the changing exigencies of the complex communication situations which he was assessing and making responsible observations and comments for the public(s) he was trying to inform and influence.

James Reston, perhaps, provides us with the first hint of whether change in approach was, indeed, an identifying characteristic of the type of discourse, *Real Advocacy Journalism*™, that Lippmann practiced. "The point is not that he [Lippmann] was never wrong or that he did not change his ideas and even on occasion contradict his own theories, but that he provoked thought, encouraged debate, forced definition and often revision of policies, and nourished the national dialogue on great subjects for over half a century."[12]

Reston goes on to observe that the method of Walter Lippmann has been "half in the noisy pit and half in the quiet study, a duality of engagement in the world of public affairs and disengagement from the world of affairs into the world of books and political philosophy, of reason and meditation on ultimate values."[13] Lippmann, himself, writes in *The Public Philosophy* of the "Two Realms." These are the realms of earth and heaven, the practical and the ethereal: "this world where the human condition is to be born, to live, to struggle and die; and the transcendent world in which men's souls can be regenerated and at peace."[14]

Lippmann worked "in the theoretical realm of the ideal society and in the more practical and mundane realm of day-to-day political problems."[15] As Lippmann, himself, once said: "I have lived two lives, one of books and one of newspapers. Each helps the other. The philosophy is the context in which I write my columns. The column is the laboratory or clinic in which I test the philosophy and keep it from becoming too abstract."[16]

Lippmann was about the business of advocating courses of action for societal problems, those of a current nature being dealt with in his column and those of a lasting nature treated in many of his books. But even in dealing with problems of society, Lippmann never deluded himself into thinking that he had or was offering a final solution or that one such solution existed. As a throwback from his days at Harvard, Lippmann realized that philosophical systems are often inadequate even though their authors may perceive them as true and binding. Lippmann said that the grandest philosophical systems or theories are more "like village lamp posts than they are like the sun." In the greatest philosophical work, only an individual is speaking. The search for the "philosopher's stone," worse than being a quest for something not to be found, represents "the old indolence of believing that somebody [has] done the world's thinking once and for all."[17] This simply is never the case is Lippmann's point.

Lippmann lived through times in which each decade had its different climate, its different crises. If his thinking had not changed with the times, it would not have kept pace with the problems and crises, and his advice or solutions would have been of no consequence.

He was well aware that the conclusions he had reached in his column on a given day were subject to revision by the news of that day.[18] Characterized as a "genuine searcher after truth," Lippmann refused to become the "prisoner of consistency." Once he was taken to task because of a reversal of position on the gold standard and he was quoted as saying, "I do not wish to pretend that in all matters, or even in all aspect of this one matter, my articles have been consistent and unchanging. I have often changed my opinions, sometimes because they appeared later to be wrong, sometimes because I have lived and learned, and sometimes, as in the case of the gold standard, because events themselves changed."[19]

Implicitly, Lippmann was saying that to offer meaningful advice, responsible comment, or solutions is to consider the times and conditions surrounding the issue or crisis at hand, whether or not they are in effect contradictory to a previous position advanced. That is characteristic of the business in which he was engaged—that of a responsible and accountable political columnist, practicing *Real Advocacy Journalism*™.

Amid the controversy over which labels or philosophical stances can be permanently assigned to Lippmann or the charge that Lippmann has been inconsistent philosophically, it is certain that he thought very hard for many years about political and governmental problems "as current as any day's headline and as old as Plato's *Republic*."[20] Clearly, he found history instructive, whether assessing philosophical tracts, political theories, seminal events, or defining periods of time.

Throughout his discourse with the American public (and other publics) his constant concern was how a democratic form of government can be conceived and applied to effectuate and promote the best life for mankind given: a) the basic nature of man; b) the problems of governing; and c) those evolutionary and inevitable changes (social, political, and economic) of society. Or, as one author puts it, "beyond the ephemeral particulars of the present, other problems, ethical, general, timeless," have occupied Lippmann—problems upon which "the contemplative have brooded over the centuries; problems dealing with the inward meaning of events rather than their outward appearance; problems involving the nature of the ideal society and the spiritual no less than political values by which the individual must live." Lippmann was "haunted by the problem Aristotle raised in the seventh book of his *Politics*—how to find a bridge between man's environment, which is complex, and his political capacity, which is simple."[21]

Lippmann saw definite problems with the principles and practices of our current system of democracy. He dealt with them extensively in his books. And when incidents and situations occurred in the daily business of governing which exemplified the inadequacy of certain fundamental tenets on which the democratic system is based, he seized the opportunity, through his column, to highlight those weaknesses and misconceived premises—hoping to enlighten both participant and observer and thereby bring about a different mode of thinking—a prerequisite for necessary changes to occur. His columns portrayed the philosophical bent(s) of his mind. The philosopher-king was an ideal in the *Republic* of Plato; the philosopher-journalist was a fact in the person of Walter Lippmann. No one could read his column "Today and Tomorrow" without sensing that his approach to the contemporary scene was different from that of other newspaper commentators.

Readers turned to Lippmann for an analysis of events rather than an account of them. They relied on him to uncover their significance. Lippmann wrote with the assumption that those who turned to him cared, as he did, for "logic and enlightenment"[22] not the drama, sensationalism, superficiality, and selfish interests that so characterize commentary today.

Many contemporary observers of Lippmann, and many who have studied him since, have said he stands apart, that there will never be another political columnist, persuader of publics, like him. It would be easy for current and future journalists, columnists/commentators to accept the notion that there will never be another Lippmann and become resigned that they could never write with such authority or amass such a loyal following. But is that really the point?

The real point is what can be learned from Lippmann. What standards can practitioners ascribe to, adhere to, commit to as they seek to promote positions that will bring about the best for mankind—at whatever level of influence one might have—no matter how large or small, no matter whether it is on a local, regional, national, or international level.

Lippmann was not perfect. He made mistakes in assumptions, interpretations, and proposed solutions during his work as a persuader of publics. The important and defining trait that holds true is the seriousness with which he took his role and his responsibilities. He strove for knowledge, objectivity, factual representation as he dedicated himself and his work toward advancing the good, the best, for society through the practice of *Real Advocacy Journalism*™.

4

THE NEED, ROLE AND FUNCTION OF REAL ADVOCACY JOURNALISM™

Walter Lippmann was convinced of the need for his role and others like him in the management of public affairs. His larger works explicitly and implicitly build a convincing case for the genre of *Real Advocacy Journalism*™ as exemplified by the role the political column/commentary plays in shaping public opinion.

During the majority of the twentieth century, the public relied primarily on newspapers for such guidance. In the twenty-first century as newspapers continue to decline in content, circulation, and reach, the public has turned more to television, radio, and the Internet, with all its online sources, to remain informed and to get direction for action.

Compelling arguments for the genre of *Real Advocacy Journalism*™ are found in four areas of his intellectual thought. In: 1) his belief in the importance of an effective system of advocatory communication as opposed to demagoguery or other coercive forces; 2) his perception of contemporary man's ability or inability, because of the nature and the complexity of the environment, to act collectively in promoting the well-being of mankind and society; 3) his assessment of what constitutes truth and knowledge for a contemporary public when, and if, it is called upon to decide the best course of action; and 4) his perception of reason, logic, facts, truth, and clear and graphic language forms as the primary and most effective instruments of public (mass) persuasion.

We turn to a more in-depth investigation into the theoretical foundation laid by Lippmann for a genre of *Real Advocacy Journalism*™ by examining his views regarding advocatory communication.

The Relationship Between Freedom of Speech and Advocacy

Lippmann's view on freedom of speech provides us with insight into his conception of the role of advocatory communication. For Lippmann, exercising the basic right of freedom of speech has advocative dimensions. When one speaks, he/she speaks with some desired end in mind. And this motivation makes the very utterance advocative. Lippmann says freedom of speech is conceived as a means of a confrontation of opinion.

To show how entrenched and pervasive, even though not often articulated, the concept of freedom of speech as being "a means to a confrontation of opinion" is in our society, Lippmann says most of our basic beliefs are formed through advocative transactions and are not exempt from continuously close scrutiny and demand for proof. The implication is that there is and should be a continuous questioning and challenging of the evidence before us on any given subject until we have attained the best proof (or substantiation for truth) possible. This is the only way man as a fallible being can hope to attain certainty about anything.

Lippmann claims that even our most basic beliefs—from scientific theories about how things work in nature to postulates regarding human social behavior—should be subjected to the process of dialectic, and to advocatory proof before they are accepted, before they become a part of the prevailing paradigm or part of that group of facts which represent knowledge or truth. Theories and premises are continuously subjected to dialectical discussion and advocatory proof as new evidence is discovered.

Beyond defining freedom of speech as having an advocatory dimension, Lippmann proceeds to advance a broader, more inclusive, more moralistic position on freedom of speech: that the mere utterance of a public statement—a statement intended for someone other than oneself—carries the obligation to subject that statement to criticism and debate in order to ascertain its validity and truth. According to Lippmann, no one can justify in principle, much less in practice, a claim that there exists an "unrestricted right of anyone to utter anything he likes at any time he chooses."[1] As an example, Lippmann says, "there can... be no right as Mr. Justice Holmes said to cry 'fire' in a crowded theatre. Nor is there a right to tell a customer that the glass beads are diamonds, or a voter that the opposition candidate for president is a Soviet agent."[2]

In essence, Lippmann posits that "the right to utter words, whether or not they have meaning, and regardless of their truth, could not be of vital interest to a great state but for the presumption that they are the chaff which goes with the utterance of true and significant words."[3]

Lippmann goes on to warn of the vulnerability of freedom of speech when the silliness, baseness, and deception becomes so dominant that the kernels of truth are submerged.[4] "If there is a dividing line between liberty and license," asserts Lippmann, "it is where freedom of speech is no longer respected as procedure of the truth and becomes the unrestricted right to exploit the ignorance, and to incite the passions, of the people."[5] In such cases freedom of speech becomes such a "hullabaloo of sophistry, propaganda, special pleading, lobbying and salesmanship that it is difficult to remember why freedom of speech is worth the pain and trouble of defending it."[6]

Lippmann observes, "but while dialectic is a process of criticism wherein lies the path to the principles of all inquiries, rhetoric [advocacy] is concerned with the modes of persuasion."[7] Lippmann goes on to speak of the importance of persuasion in contemporary society: "Within the life of the generation now in control of public affairs, persuasion has become a self-conscious art and a regular organ of popular government. None of us begins to understand the consequences, but it is no daring prophecy to say that the knowledge of how to create consent will alter every political calculation and modify every political premise."[8]

Lippmann is saying here that public persuasion, as a "self-conscious" art or as a preoccupation on the part of popular governments, became more prevalent, and necessarily so, during the twentieth century than at any other time in the history of popular and democratic forms of government. This is true, according to Lippmann, because "under the impact of propaganda, not necessarily in the sinister meaning of the word alone, the old constants of our thinking have become variables. It is no longer possible, for example, to believe in the original dogma of democracy; that the knowledge needed for the management of human affairs comes up spontaneously from the heart."[9] This observation is also relevant in the twenty-first century.

According to Lippmann, it cannot be assumed that man has been endowed with some special insight to manage the affairs of government automatically. Unfortunately, the wisdom, foresight, and know-how in managing government did not come along with the sovereignty which grants man the ultimate right to determine government's form. How to manage human affairs cannot be based on insight or some other abstractions. He warns that "where we act on that theory we expose ourselves to self-deception, and to forms of persuasion that we cannot verify."[10] He asserts firmly, "it has been demonstrated that we cannot rely on intuition, conscience or the accidents or casual opinion if we are to deal with the world beyond our reach."[11]

Lippmann is very aware that persuasion (or the "manufacture of consent" as he calls it) as an art has existed through the ages, but it has undergone great refinements. Such refinements have far-reaching implications for the current practice of democracy. He acknowledges the intricacy of the process by which public opinion is shaped. Opportunities for manipulation are open to anyone who understands the process. "The creation of consent," says Lippmann, "is not a new art." It simply has "improved enormously in technic."[12] It is now based on "analysis rather than rule of thumb. And so, as a result of psychological research, coupled with the modern means of communication, the practice of democracy has turned a corner. A revolution is taking place infinitely more significant than any shifting of economic power."[13]

This is seen in the role and charge of public officials. "In the prevailing view," Lippmann says, "they [public officials, leaders, advisors, all public persons of influence] are the agents of destiny. It is they, or others panting to take their places, who are to contrive the shape of things to come. They are to breed a better race of men. They are to arrange abundance for all. They are to abolish classes. They are to take charge of the present. They are to conceive the future. They are to plan the activities of mankind. They are to manage its labors. They are to formulate its culture. They are to establish convictions."[14] But most importantly, "they can accomplish," says Lippmann, "*only what they can command or persuade* an unseen multitude to do."[15] (Emphasis added).

Lippmann believed that the good of democratic society can be advanced through a system of public communication only if that system is based on the precept that freedom of speech is "a means to a confrontation of opinion" where the methods of dialectic and the art of advocacy play critical roles in ascertaining and promoting the truth. For Lippmann, freedom of speech "can be justified, applied, regulated in a plural society only by adhering to the postulate that there is a rational order of things in which it is possible, by sincere inquiry and rational debate, to distinguish the true and the false, the right and the wrong, the good which leads to the destruction and to the death of civility."[16]

Lippmann readily reminds us that our free institutions were conceived and established on the belief that "all issues could be settled by scientific investigation and free debate if—but only if—all the investigators and the debaters adhered to the public philosophy of using the same criteria and rules of reason for arriving at the truth and for distinguishing good and evil."[17]

Lippmann goes on to say that "because the confrontation is to discern truth, there are rules of evidence and of parliamentary procedure, there are codes of fair dealing and fair comment, by which a loyal man will consider himself bound when he exercises the right to publish opinions."[18]

Lippmann stresses that "without protection against propaganda, without standards of evidence, without criteria of emphasis, the living substance of all popular decision is exposed to every prejudice and to infinite exploitation."[19] The method of dialectic, as a critical part of the public communication process, is to provide the protection and the means by which to ascertain truth. The art of advocacy—the counterpart of dialectic—is available in that it can promote truth and move masses toward truth's end through the process and techniques of persuasion.

With Lippmann's conviction of the importance of advocacy in the process of public communication, we have our first indication of a need for *Real Advocacy Journalism*™. Such a genre of discourse can provide the necessary debate or dialogue regarding any action or policy advanced for public consumption or public purpose. The advocate journalist through a daily newspaper column (now, also commentary on radio, TV, and online) for example, could perform both a dialectical and advocatory function by placing the issue(s) of the day in perspective, as he/she stimulates thought and gives direction by discussing the relevant sides of the issue and urging the alignment of the public with a particular side.

We see an even more pressing need for *Real Advocacy Journalism*™ as Lippmann assesses contemporary man's inability to formulate his own opinions on issues, considering the complex and demanding nature of his environment. Lippmann shows how the vastness and complexity of contemporary society no longer allow the dialectical process to take place on a broad scale; and many issues facing contemporary man on any given day cannot in a practical sense be subjected to the rigorous inquiry of truth. Therefore, contemporary man must rely on someone to discover what the truth is, convey it to him so that he can act or respond responsibly. That someone is the advocate journalist, the political columnist, the commentator—committed and engaged in the practice of *Real Advocacy Journalism*™.

Contemporary Man's Ability to Make Responsible Decisions As a Collective

Lippmann's perception of contemporary man's ability to act responsibly as a collective is a further indication of the need for a genre of discourse such as *Real Advocacy Journalism*™. Lippmann examines contemporary man's ability to act as a collective in reference to his complex environment.

In fact, for Lippmann, an assessment or characterization of the nature of contemporary man can only be made against the backdrop of contemporary society. Contemporary man is as complex as his environment. He is at once forced to be a part of a private, self-contained, self-centered, manageable community as well as part of a distant, multi-faceted, multi-cultured, unmanageable, and to a great extent, invisible world. Basically, the world that contemporary man has to deal with, according to Lippmann, is "out of reach, out of sight, out of mind. It is to be explored, reported, and imagined."[20]

There is a basic condition of contemporary society in which "each of us lives and works on a small part of the earth's surface, moves in a small circle, and of these acquaintances knows only a few intimately." And "of any public event that has wide effects, we see at best only a phase and an aspect.... Inevitably our opinions cover a bigger space, a longer reach of time, a greater number of things than we can directly observe. They have, therefore, to be pieced together out of what others have reported and what we can imagine."[21]

Therefore, contemporary man is often forced to function with an incomplete and often distorted picture of reality. There are several factors inherent in the structure of contemporary society which limit contemporary man's direct access to the facts. They are "artificial censorships, the limitations of social contact, the comparatively meager time available in each day for paying attention to public affairs, the distortion arising because events have to be compressed into very short messages, the difficulty of making a small vocabulary express a complicated world and finally the fear of facing those facts which would seem to threaten the established routine in men's lives."[22]

Contemporary man, because of his environment, also relies very heavily on stereotypes. "We are told about the world before we see it. We imagine most things before we experience them"[23] Unless we have become informed by some educational process, we are governed by those preconceptions provided to us.

Preconceptions "mark out certain objects as familiar or strange, emphasizing the difference, so that the slightly familiar is seen as very familiar, and the somewhat strange as sharply alien. They are aroused by small signs which may vary from a true index to a vague analogy. Aroused, they flood fresh vision with older images, and project into the world what has been resurrected in memory."[24] Stereotypes acquired from earlier experiences are more often than not carried over into judgment of later ones.[25] And, according to Lippmann, "the subtlest and most pervasive of all influences are those which create and maintain the repertory of stereotypes."[26]

The tendency for contemporary man to rely on stereotypes, more so than ancient Athenians functioning in the Greek city-states during Aristotle's time, is due to the hurried and multi-various nature of contemporary society. Unlike ancient Greek society, today for example, physical distance separates men who are often in vital contact with each other, such as, employer and employee, official and voter. "There is neither time nor opportunity for intimate acquaintance. Instead, contemporary man will notice a trait which marks a well-known type, and fill in the rest of the picture by means of a stereotype he carries about in his head,"[27]

Lippmann gives several examples: "He is an agitator. That much we notice or are told. Well, an agitator is this sort of person, and so he is this sort of person." Again, "he is an intellectual. He is a plutocrat. He is a foreigner. He is a 'South European.'" And again, "he is from Back Bay. He is a Harvard man. How different from the statement: He is a Yale man. He is a regular fellow. He is a West Pointer. He is an old army sergeant. He is a Greenwich Villager: what don't we know about him then, and about her?"[28] Other contemporary examples include: He is a southerner; he is a communist; he is a native New Yorker, he is from Iowa; he/she is a racist, conservative, liberal, and so on.

Contemporary man's use of stereotypes to order and manage his environment has both good and bad side effects. "Were there no practical uniformities in the environment" Lippmann acknowledges, "there would be no economy and only error in the human habit of accepting foresight for sight. But there are uniformities sufficiently accurate, and the need of economizing attention is so inevitable, that the abandonment of all stereotypes for a wholly innocent approach to experience would impoverish human life."[29]

What is important is "the character of the stereotypes" and the gullibility with which contemporary man employs them. The character and gullibility of the stereotypes, fundamentally, depend upon those inclusive patterns which constitute one's perception and/or philosophy of life. If in that perception or philosophy contemporary man assumes that the world is codified only according to a code he possesses, then he is likely to make his assessments of what is going on and describe a world run by his code, only.

But, if his perception or philosophy tells him that each man is only a small part of a larger world, that his intelligence, his ability, catches at best only phases and aspects in a coarse limited net of ideas, then, when he uses his stereotypes, he will tend to know that they are only stereotypes, and that they should be held lightly, and he should willingly modify them if necessary.[30]

If the later philosophical posture or tendency is adhered to, then contemporary man would realize more and more clearly when his ideas started, where they started, how they came to him, and why he accepted them. Likewise, he will realize when and how they need to be modified, totally discarded, and abandoned. Lippmann says, "All useful history is antiseptic in this fashion. It enables us to know what fairy tale, what schoolbook, what tradition, what novel, play, picture, phrase, planted one preconception in this mind, another in that mind."[31]

For Lippmann, what the contemporary advocate journalist must always be mindful of is how "messages from the outside are affected by the stored up images, the preconceptions, and prejudices which interpret them, fill them out, and in their turn powerfully direct the play of our attention, and our vision itself."[32]

Lippmann's assessment of the nature of contemporary man is a radical departure from the treatment of man's nature by the classical advocatory theorists in terms of focus. We cannot view contemporary man's nature separately and distinct from his environment. But classical theorists, because of the relative simplicity and homogeneity of ancient society (and to lesser extent medieval society), could afford to confine their treatment of human nature to biological (drives) and the psychological (emotions) aspects of man during various stages of the life cycle, as Aristotle did in the *Rhetoric*, and virtually ignore the environmental factors influencing him.

But what one gathers from Lippmann is that an advocate journalist today can ill-afford to consider just the various emotional aspects of man's nature, his biological drives, or his virtues as Aristotle and other traditional theorists did. There are too many environmental forces acting upon contemporary man, which cannot be ignored, forces that his ancient, medieval, and modern predecessors did not encounter or have to cope with as they functioned in their societies. The advocate journalist must look at how beliefs are formed—how contemporary man's environment and culture influence him.

According to Lippmann, men act on pseudo-environments—the formulation of some interior representations of the world.[33] And the pseudo-environment is a hybrid compounded of "human nature" and "conditions."[34]

The important thing to note is "the very fact men theorize at all is proof that their pseudo-environments, their interior representations of the world, are a determining element in thought, feeling and action. For, if the connection between reality and human response were direct and immediate, rather than indirect and inferred, indecision and failure would be unknown...."[35]

If this is the case, Lippmann does not define the nature of contemporary man as consisting of fixed identifiable traits which are immune to environmental impact and, which can always be used to predict human behavior. For Lippmann, there is no such accurate and well-defined picture of human nature.

Furthermore, for him "there is no one self always at work. And, therefore, it is of great importance in the formation of any public opinion, what self is engaged."[36]

From contemporary psychology we have learned to note many or "multiple selves," within the individual. "We understand that we see the same body, but often a different man, depending on whether he is dealing with a social equal, a social inferior, or a social superior; ... or whether he is dealing with his children, his partners, his most trusted subordinates, the boss who can make him or break him; or whether he is struggling for the necessities of life, or successful; or whether he is dealing with a foreign alien, or a despised one; or whether he is in great danger, or in perfect security; or whether he is alone in Paris or among his family in Peoria."[37]

The selves that we, along with other influences, construct "prescribe which impulses, how emphasized, how directed, are appropriate to certain typical situations for which we have learned prepared attitudes. For a recognizable type of experience, there is a character which controls the outward manifestations of our whole being."[38]

What is critical and what the contemporary advocacy journalist must always be mindful of is that as he/she moves from generalities to details in his/her analysis of the nature of contemporary man, it becomes more apparent that the character in which men deal with their affairs is not fixed. "Possibly their different selves have a common stem and common qualities, but the branches and the twigs have many forms. Nobody confronts every situation with the same character. His character varies in some degree through the sheer influence of time and accumulating memory since he is not an automation. His character varies, not only in time, but according to circumstance."[39] And to reiterate, Lippmann says "there is no one self at work. And, therefore, it is of great importance in the formation of any public opinion, what self is engaged."[40]

Lippmann's theory that the nature of contemporary man is characterized by a manifestation of "multiple selves" is not only a plausible explanation of how man adapts to his multi-faceted environment—with its many, varied, and often diametrically opposed demands—but it is also indicative of Lippmann's attempt to resolve the age-old philosophical problem regarding the inherent duality of man's nature—the problem of good and evil. Lippmann is very aware of how this duality in man's nature has determined his behavior at critical moments in history. For example, in the instance of war, the evil, the worst aspects of man's nature are brought to bear. In such instances, Lippmann sees the traditional ideal of what he calls "civility"—the ideal that there exists a standard of public and private conduct which promotes, facilitates, and protects the overall well-being of society—discarded.

Lippmann, therefore, needs a theory of human nature which will at once enable him to maintain the belief that the ideal of civility is still viable as well as explain its lapse in time of war. A theory which fails to sustain the ideal of civility would leave Lippmann cynical as a public communicator. Likewise, the theory which fails to explain the apparent absence of the ideal make him naive.

Lippmann's theory of multiple selves allows him to deal with the problem of evil in man's nature as he maintains faith in the ideal of civility. More importantly, his theory allows him to believe that man, because of the tendency to take on different characters, is not immune to persuasion and guidance as to what constitutes the proper course of action in various situations.

Lippmann's theory of "multiple selves" also helps to explain, and perhaps reconcile the conflict presented by the concepts of public and private selves. If the public communicator can believe in the theory of multiple selves, then such a theory accounts for the natural co-existence of a public and private self. Distinctions, qualifications, and analysis regarding this dichotomy in man are made by the public communicator only in an attempt to persuade. The advocate journalist must be aware of both the public and private self, and he must make the necessary adjustments based on which self he seeks to engage for persuasion as well as on what issue(s) and under what circumstances he seeks to persuade.

Lippmann has based his theory of multiple selves on the premise that environmental and social circumstances in contemporary society force man to assume many characters in an attempt to cope with and manage his surroundings, his life. And Lippmann's concept of man acting in a pseudo-environment can be interpreted as man's attempt to resolve the inner conflict brought about by the public and private aspect of his life. The pseudo-environments are representative of a meshing, an assimilation, an ordering of the frequent conflicting roles and their corresponding demands accompanying public and private expectations.

An awareness, on the part of the political columnist/commentator, the advocate journalist, of both notions of multiple selves and pseudo-environments are paramount to Lippmann's system of *Real Advocacy Journalism*™.

Another perspective of Lippmann's, which is paramount and supports the concept of *Real Advocacy Journalism*™ is the idea that what constitutes knowledge for contemporary man is more often than not inadequate. Therefore, a man, for the most part, is incapable of making intelligent decisions regarding public policies on the one hand and private concerns on the other. The complexities of society have forced him to look to other experts, the advisors, for knowledge and direction. Philosophically, Lippmann is advancing an anti-populist, eighteenth-century, aristocratic position. He is explicit in rejecting the premise that the people are in a position to serve as reliable guides in the formulation of public policy. He also rejects the notion that their spontaneous opinions are reliable indicators as to what should be the proper course of action in any given issue.

In an interview with the author, James Reston said of Lippmann: "He believed in the education of the masses, but he didn't believe in the judgment of the masses. He was not essentially a democrat. He believed in the kind of people, the special elites that were in a position to have adequate information to make the right judgements and decisions. He did not think that people were qualified to pass judgment on what, for example, should be done about the MX missile. Should it be one bomb? What should we do about Poland? How should we deal with Afghanistan, the hostages, Tehran? And he was probably right about that."[41]

Contemporary man's environment for the most part, according to Lippmann, is invisible and too complex for him personally to acquire knowledge and understanding of how it works or in all cases what is needed to make it work. Having access to self-evident truths, and empirically verifiable facts is not a common occurrence in contemporary man's everyday activities. He simply cannot experience events first-hand. His world is too vast and too out of reach. So, he must rely on the only means for gaining access to the invisible elements of his environment, mass media. But mass media, by their very nature and technical structure, can only present bits and pieces of what actually occurs. Too often, because of the time limitations and arbitrary censorships of the media, contemporary man receives as knowledge incomplete facts to explain a scientific phenomenon, or selected pictures to explain an occurrence.

As a result of his inadequate access to first-hand data, contemporary man turns and, more importantly, should turn to the experts, the advisors—those people who can provide the necessary guidance, knowledge, and truth. This is true for the man of public affairs as well as for the average citizen. He looks to the people he considers authorities or experts to help him make an informed decision, the right decision.

Lippmann warns the advocate journalist, the public communicator, that the dialectical process for arriving at truth can only be used effectively on a small scale in today's society. The technical nature of mass media does not lend itself well to the methods of dialectic. For all the points of view media advance, and in the many avenues that advance them, it is impossible to advance equitably the opposite points of view. And the true dialectical process breaks down. The best that can be hoped for is that in instances where there is no agreement among the experts as to what is the proper course of action, dialectic and debate can occur among the experts. This exchange can be viewed by large publics, audiences, providing an opportunity to have access to the same information, often at the same time.

What Constitutes Public Knowledge

What constitutes knowledge and truth for contemporary man, according to Lippmann, is also determined to a great degree by the structure and nature of contemporary society. The world, about which each man is supposed to have knowledge, has become so complicated as to defy his powers of understanding.

What contemporary man knows of events that matter enormously to him—as the purposes of governments, the aspirations of peoples, the struggles of classes—he knows at second, third, or fourth hand. He cannot observe everything for himself. Even the things that are near to him so often become too involved for his judgment.[42] "I know of no man, says Lippmann, "even among those who devote all of their time to watching public affairs, who can even pretend to keep track, at the same time, of his city government, Congress, the department, the industrial situation, and the rest of the world. What men who make the study of politics [and Lippmann defines politics as the science of public affairs] a vocation cannot do, the man who has an hour a day for newspapers and talk cannot possibly hope to do. He must seize catchwords and headlines or nothing."[43]

So, immediately, we can discard any notion about truth being spontaneous, or "that the means of securing truth exist when there is no external interference" or that "the truth about distant or complex matters is self-evident."[44] Such assumptions would be false in dealing with an invisible environment such as we have in contemporary society.

The real problem of what constitutes knowledge for contemporary man lies in the means by which an invisible world is made visible to him. The primary vehicle is the media, both print and electronic. "Universally it is admitted that the press is the chief means of contact with the unseen environment. And practically everywhere it is assumed that the press should do spontaneously for us what primitive democracy imagined each of us could do spontaneously for himself, that every day and twice a day it will present us with a true picture of all the outer world in which we are interested."[45] This is a false assumption. The news cannot be relied upon to provide either complete knowledge (all the facts about an event) or the total truth (an accurate picture of an occurrence). The news, for example, "does not tell you how the seed is germinating in the ground, but it may tell you when the first sprout breaks through the surface... it may tell you that the sprout did not come up at the time it was expected."[46]

The point is that the news is not a very good source of knowledge. It does not report all the facts because of a number of reasons: time limitations, complexity of the facts involved, and censorship, to name a few. Furthermore, the facts which are reported cannot be treated as synonymous with truth. "Were reporting the simple recovery of obvious facts, the press agent would be little more than a clerk. But since, in respect to most of the big topics of news, the facts are not simple, and not at all obvious, but subject to choice and opinion, it is natural that everyone should wish to make his choice of facts for the newspaper print."[47] The publicity man does that, according to Lippmann.

The publicity man "is the censor and propagandist, responsible only to his employers, and to the whole truth responsible only as it accords with the employers' conception of his own interest."[48] More importantly, "the development of the publicity man is a clear sign that the facts of modern life do not spontaneously take a shape in which they can be known."[49] Therefore, by the time the newspaper reaches the reader, it "is the result of a whole series of selections as to what items shall be printed, how much space each shall occupy, what emphasis each shall have. There are no objective standards here. There are conventions."[50] Lippmann gives an example: "Take two newspapers published in the same city on the same morning. The headline of one reads: 'Britain pledges aid to Berlin against French Aggression; France openly backs Poles.' The headline of the second is 'Mrs. Stillman's Other Love.' Which you prefer is a matter of taste, but not entirely a matter of the editor's taste. It is a matter of his judgment as to what will absorb the half hour's attention a certain set of readers will give to his newspaper."[51]

So, Lippmann continues, "if we assume...that news and truth are two words for the same thing, we shall, I believe, arrive nowhere. The best that news can do is to signalize an event." While the function of truth is "to bring to light the hidden facts, to set them into relation with each other and to make a picture of reality on which men can act."[52]

Unfortunately, the truth cannot be easily arrived at or easily obtained for the mass of contemporary men. There are practical problems. For example, "the modern media of mass communication does not lend itself easily to a confrontation of opinion. The dialectical process for finding truth works best when the same audience hears all sides of the disputation."[53] This is manifestly impossible in contemporary society because of the many forms which messages take and the many ways in which they are transmitted as representative of the truth in mass media.

Take movies and films: "If a film advocates a thesis, the same audience cannot be shown another film designed to answer it. Radio and television broadcasts do permit debate. Despite the effort to let opposing views be heard equally, and to organize programs on which there are opposing speakers, the technical conditions of broadcasting do not favor genuine and productive debate. For the audience, turning on and turning off here and there, cannot be counted upon to hear even in summary form, the essential evidence and the main arguments on all the significant sides of a question."[54] Lippmann continues, "rarely, and on very few public issues does the mass audience have the benefit of the process by which truth is sifted from error— the dialectic of debate in which there is immediate challenge, reply, cross examination, and rebuttal."[55] The fact of the matter is "the men who regularly broadcast the news and comment upon the news cannot—like a speaker in the Senate or in the House of Commons—be challenged by one of their listeners and compelled then and there to verify their statements of fact and to re-argue their inferences from the facts."[56]

What contemporary man has failed to remember is that the press is no substitute for institutions. Rather, the press is "like a beam of a searchlight that moves restlessly about, bringing one episode and then another out of darkness into vision." But "men cannot do the work of the world by this light alone. They cannot govern society by episodes, incidents, and eruptions. It is only when they work by a steady light of their own, that the press, when it is turned upon them, reveals a situation intelligible enough for a popular decision."[57]

Lippmann is saying here that truth or knowledge regarding anything cannot be acquired or conveyed at a glance. The whole picture, all facts and circumstances must somehow be apprehended and conveyed if true knowledge is to be required. The documentary would probably be the most representative example for Lippmann of knowledge being gathered and conveyed methodically, fairly, and thoroughly by mass media today.

But the trouble with mass knowledge goes deeper than the problems of mass media, and so does the remedy. The problem, according to Lippmann, "lies in social organization based on a system of analysis and record, and in all the corollaries of that principle; in the abandonment of the theory of the omni-competent citizen, in the decentralization of decision, in the coordination of decision by comparable record and analysis. If at the centers of management there is a running audit, which makes work intelligible to those who do it, and those who pretend it, issues when they arise are not the mere collisions of the blind. Then, too, the news is uncovered for the press by a system of intelligence that is also a check upon the press."[58]

For, basically, the troubles of the press go back to a common source: "to the failure of self-governing people to transcend their casual experience and their prejudice, by inventing, creating, and organizing a machinery of knowledge."[59] And, Lippmann observes, "it is because they are compelled to act without a reliable picture of the world, that governments, schools, newspapers and churches make such a small headway against the more obvious failings of democracy, against violent prejudice, apathy, preference for the curious trivial as against the dull important, and the hunger, for sideshows and three-legged calves. This is the primary defect of popular government, a defect inherent in its traditions, and all its other defects can, I believe, be traced to this one."[60]

The problems of imparting knowledge to the mass of contemporary men have been difficult.

The people who break down the drama of occurrences, break through the stereotypes contemporary man harbors, and instead offer him a picture of facts, are the experts. "Every complicated community has sought the assistance of special men, of augurs, priests, elders." Our own democracy, Lippmann reminds us, is "based on a theory of universal competence, sought lawyers to manage its government, and to help manage its industry." It has long been recognized that the specially trained man is in some way "oriented to a wider system of truth than which arises spontaneously in the amateur's mind."[61]

Experience has shown that the traditional lawyer's expertise is insufficient. "The Great Society," says Lippmann, "had grown furiously and to colossal dimensions by the application of technical knowledge. It was made by engineers who had learned to use exact measurements and quantitative analysis. It could not be governed, men began to discover, by men who thought deductively about rights and wrongs. It could be brought under human control only by the technic, which had created it."[62]

Given these conditions, "the more enlightened minds have called in experts who were trained, or had trained themselves, to make parts of his Great Society intelligible to those who manage it."[63] The expert "becomes the man who prepares the facts for the men of action.... He no longer stands outside, chewing the cud provided by busy men of affairs," rather "he takes his place in front of decision instead of behind it."[64]

It must be conceded by contemporary society that "all forms of human association must, because of sheer practical difficulty, contain men who will come to see the need for an expert reporting of their particular environment."[65]

The expert is the intermediary between contemporary man and his massive and complex environment; he is the key to knowledge and the management of it. And if we look about us, we will see that the wedge has been driven by many men of public affairs: by directors of industry, and statesmen who needed help, by the bureaus of municipal research, by the legislative reference libraries, by the specialized lobbies of corporations and trade unions and public causes, and by voluntary organizations like the League of Women Voters, the National Organization of Women, the Consumer's League, the American Civil Liberties Union, the Manufacturers' Association, the AFL-CIO; by hundreds of trade associations, and citizens' unions; and by many publications and foundations. All of them have begun to "demonstrate the need for interposing some form of expertness between the private citizen and the vast environment in which he is entangled."[66]

Even out of the realm of public affairs, contemporary man on a smaller scale, during events in his daily life, looks to the experts for clues, for guidance. He makes his connections with the outer world through "certain beloved and authoritative persons. They are the first bridge to the invisible world."[67] And though he may gradually master for himself many phases of that larger environment, there always remains a vaster one that is unknown, which contemporary man relates through authorities. When and where all the facts are out of sight, a true report and a false one read alike, sound alike. Except on a few subjects where his knowledge is great, contemporary man cannot choose between true and false accounts. So, he chooses between trustworthy and untrustworthy authorities or experts.[68]

In actuality, "on all but a few matters for very short stretches in our lives, the utmost independence that we can exercise is to multiply the authorities to whom we give a friendly hearing. As congenital amateurs, our quest for truth consists in stirring up the experts and forcing them to answer any heresy that has the accent of conviction. In such a debate we can often judge who has won the dialectical victory, but we are virtually defenseless against a false premise that none of the debaters has challenged, or a neglected aspect that none of them has brought into argument."[74]

Lippmann has clearly established that contemporary man, without experts, other figures considered authorities, is in no position to have an informed opinion or make an intelligent decision on very many important issues. He must rely on such experts and advisors to present him with accurate pictures of the reality he himself cannot witness, comprehend, or master in its actual state of being. It must be comprehended, mastered, and put into perspective for him. Only then can he begin to deal efficiently with it.

Lippmann has built a convincing case as to why the typical citizen needs an intermediary in managing the public affairs that have a direct impact on his/her life, and that of his/her community and country. Furthermore, Lippmann builds a case as to why accurate, balanced, and understandable communication is so critical in preparing the average, busy, personally absorbed citizen to be able to arrive at the right decision when called upon in the public policy process.

Lippmann also signals the importance of the proper and effective use of language in the public communication, public persuasion process, in carrying out *Real Advocacy Journalism*™.

Required Use of Graphic Language and Language Forms

Lippmann's life-long work is testimony to the value he assigns language and language forms in moving men toward a desired course of action. Besides his own effective use of language, Lippmann is explicit, in more than one instance, about the effective use of words as the prime vehicle for communicating in contemporary society.

In Lippmann's opinion, there should be rigorous discipline in the use of words. "It is almost impossible to overestimate," says Lippmann, "the confusion in daily life caused by sheer inability to use language with intention."[70] He goes on to say, we make talk scornfully of "mere words", but it is through words the whole vast process of human communication takes place. The sights, the sounds, and meanings of nearly all that we deal with as politics, "we learn, not by our own experience, but through the words of others."[71] And, "if those words are meaningless limps charged with emotion, instead of the messengers of fact, all sense of evidence breaks down."[72]

Words convey meanings, ideas; they conjure pictures in the mind. They are symbols and they create symbols, and symbols are "an important part of the machinery of human communication."[73] Most importantly, for the advocate journalist as persuader of public(s), symbols—be they the creation of a single word or a grouping of words—play a major role in the persuasion process in contemporary society, on an individual level as well as when it is necessary to persuade the masses.

The offering of symbols is generous and the meaning that can be assigned or conveyed is elastic. How then does any symbol take root in any particular person's mind? One way, according to Lippmann, is that "it is planted there by another human being whom we recognize as authoritative." And, "if it is planted deeply enough, it may be that later we shall call the person authoritative who waves that symbol at us. But in the first instance, symbols are made congenial and important because they are introduced to us by congenial and important people."[74]

We also, as individuals making untrained observations, pick recognizable signs out of the environment. "The signs stand for ideas, and these ideas we fill out with our stock of images. We do not so much see this man and that sunset; rather we notice that the things are a man or a sunset and then see chiefly what our mind is already full of on those subjects."[75]

Words, signs, and symbols kindle reactions within us. "The same word will connote any number of different ideas: emotions are displaced from the images to which they belong, to names which resemble the names of these images."[76]

The point Lippmann makes is that within limits, the emotion is transferable both in regard to stimulus and response. So, if among a number of people who possess various tendencies to respond, one can find a stimulus which will arouse the same emotion in many of them, he can substitute it for the original stimulus. Writing in 1922, Lippmann uses this example: "if... one man dislikes the League, another hates Mr. Wilson, and a third fears labor, you may be able to unite them if you can find some symbol which is the antithesis of what they all hate. Suppose that symbol is Americanism. The first man may read it as meaning the preservation of American isolation, or he may call it independence; the second as the rejection of a politician who clashes with his ideas of what an American president should be; the third as a cause to resist revolution." The point is, "the symbol itself signifies literally no one thing in particular, but it can be associated with almost anything. And because of that it can become the common bond of common feelings, even though those feelings were originally attached to disparate ideas."[77] That is how words, which stand for symbols, which stand for ideas stimulate certain feelings within individuals to bring about a common reaction.

The same principle holds where a common feeling is to be generated among the masses. And it is, perhaps, in the persuasion of the masses, where the use of symbols is so valuable. Lippmann says, "…where masses of people must cooperate in an uncertain and eruptive environment, it is usually necessary to secure unity and flexibility without real consent."[78] The symbol does just that, according to Lippmann. "It obscures personal intention, neutralizes discrimination, and obfuscates individual purpose. It immobilizes personality, yet at the same time it enormously sharpens the intention of the group and welds that group, as nothing else in a crisis can weld it, to purposeful action."[79] What is critically important about the function of the symbol is that it "renders the mass mobile though it immobilizes personality." It is "the instrument by which, in the short run, the mass escapes from its own inertia, the inertia of indecision, or the inertia of headlong movement and is rendered capable of being led along the zigzag of a complex situation."[80]

Lippmann observes that no successful leader has ever been too busy to cultivate the symbols which organize his following. "What privileges do within the hierarchy, symbols do for the rank and file. They conserve unity. From the totem pole to the national flag, from the wooden idol to God the invisible King … symbols have been cherished by leaders, many of whom were themselves unbelieved, because they were focal points where differences merged."[81]

But the smart leader knows by experience that "only when symbols have done their work is there a handle he can use to move a crowd." For it is in the symbol that "emotion is discharged at a common target and the idiosyncrasy of real ideas blotted out…" For "poking about with clear definitions and candid statements serves all high purposes known to man except the easy conversation of common will. Poking about, as every responsible leader suspects, tends to break the transference of emotion from the individual mind to the institutional symbol." And the first result of that is "chaos of individualism and warring sects. The disintegration of a symbol ... is always the beginning of a long upheaval."[82]

Because of a symbol's power to siphon emotion out of distinct ideas, Lippmann warns that the symbol is "both a mechanism of solidarity, and a mechanism of exploitation." It enables people to work for a common end, but since the few who are strategically placed must choose the concrete objectives, the symbol is also an "instrument by which a few can fatten on many, select criticism, and seduce men into facing agony, for objects they do not understand."[83] Because of this tendency, many aspects of contemporary man's subjection to symbols are not flattering if he chooses to think of himself as realistic, self-sufficient, and self-governing.

But it is impossible to conclude that symbols are altogether instruments of the unscrupulous. "In the realm of science and contemplation," says Lippmann, "they are undoubtedly the tempter himself. But in the world of action, they may be beneficent, and are sometimes a necessity. The necessity is often imagined, the peril manufactured. But when quick results are imperative, the manipulation of masses through symbols may be the only quick way of having a critical thing done."[84]

When political leaders, newspaper, or electronic media advocate things such as Americanism, Conservatism, Human Rights, "they hope to amalgamate the emotion of conflicting factions which would surely divide if, instead of these symbols, they were invited to discuss a specific program. For when a coalition around the symbol has been affected, feelings flow toward conformity under the symbol rather than toward scrutiny of the measures."[85]

Lippmann goes on to say, "it is convenient and technically correct to call multiple phrases like these symbolic. They do not stand for specific ideas, but for a sort of truce or junction between ideas. They are like a strategic railroad center where many roads converge regardless of their ultimate origin or their ultimate destination."[86] And, "he who captures the symbols by which public feeling is for the moment contained, controls by that much the approach of public policy.... A leader or an interest that can make itself master of current symbols is master of the current situation."[87]

Symbols are indeed powerful elements of persuasion—particularly persuasion of the masses. Through a process of identification with, or the stimulation of stored images and ideas, the symbol also affects the individual. But what the contemporary advocatory practitioner gathers from Lippmann is that the use of the symbol may be one of the most effective techniques of public persuasion in contemporary society because of its structure and the mass of men to be persuaded—men, each of whom having a different inclination to act, each motivated by a different set of experiences, each having a different degree of access to information, and each viewing the world through a different set of stereotypes. The use of persuasive symbols may be the only means to unite such a diverse group of audiences behind a single cause within a short or limited span of time.

By implication, Lippmann reserved the more deliberate uses of language—the construction of logical arguments, lucid analogies and, generally, language which is more precise in its meaning and direction—for the persuasion of smaller audiences, with more homogeneous orientations.

Role and Characteristics of Real Advocacy Journalism™

Lippmann's concept of public communication and the central role a system of *Real Advocacy Journalism*™ plays in it is based on the belief that freedom of speech is "the means to a confrontation of opinion." Inherent in this conception is that the very act of communicating publicly is an advocatory act. One utters public statements with the understanding that they should be subjected to debate and the methods of dialectic to ascertain their truth and validity.

To promote the truth, Lippmann emphasizes the importance of persuasion. The knowledge of how to "create consent" will alter every social and political calculation in contemporary society. Since the art of persuasion has "improved enormously in technic" and is now based on analysis rather than rule of thumb, a revolution in social control is taking place which is "infinitely more significant than any shifting of economic power." In the final analysis, public officials, and world leaders, can accomplish only what they can command or persuade an unseen multitude to do.

Lippmann also deals with the problems of the system of public communication in the twentieth century and by implication in the twenty-first century, especially those caused by man's complex and massive environment. Contemporary man's nature is no longer as simple or as easy to analyze as it was during the time of Aristotle and the Greek state. Therefore, Lippmann has advanced the theories of multiple selves and the concept of pseudo-environments to explain the nature of contemporary man and the impact of his environment upon his behavior.

The advent and technical nature of mass media have also affected communication. Mass media have made the world visible to contemporary man. Mass media are man's contact, his only experience with the world beyond his reach. But by this very nature, mass media have altered what constitutes truth and knowledge for man, for the public. The average man is not in a position to deal with empirically verifiable or self-evident truths. The media, more often than not, are his only access to the facts of a situation, and his experience or picture of an event or happening is only what the media have presented him.

Too often the facts and the picture presented are incomplete and distorted because of the nature of the medium. The technical nature of mass media also does not lend itself well to the methods of dialectic on a broad enough and meaningful scale. Consequently, as the primary source of knowledge and truth, contemporary man has turned to the expert for guidance on a personal as well as public level. He must rely on someone other than himself to tell him what the truth is. This is so because the environment has become too massive, too complex, too compartmentalized to manage.

And finally, the accurate effective use of language is the key in Lippmann's concept of public communication. James Reston said of Lippmann in an interview with the author, "he believed entirely on the written word...." Words, the meaning, the images, and the ideas they are capable of conveying, cannot be underestimated. They form the very foundation of our communication process, and it is through their manipulation that persuasion takes place among men.

We see the importance Lippmann placed on discussion and debate, and the effective use of language in governing society. An effective system of persuasive communication is paramount. More importantly, however, we see in Lippmann a need for a special type of persuasive discourse within that communication system if that system is to remain viable in fostering the well-being of society.

Because of the complexity of contemporary man's environment, because of his inability to manage it based on the information at his disposal, because of his preoccupation with the private aspects and demands of his life, and because whether prepared or not he is periodically called upon to make decisions on public matters, there is a need for discourse which will address such matters and lend direction to the public who must decide. For Lippmann, that genre of discourse is what we call *Real Advocacy Journalism*™.

There is a pressing need for someone to order, to interpret, to synthesize, to judge those events, issues, and matters in contemporary man's environment. Contemporary man needs to be prepared to think along the proper lines, and to respond intelligently when called upon. He must be advised. He must be told what thoughts to think and what actions are good. It is through *Real Advocacy Journalism*™—which is an attempt to pull everything together in order to arrive at the factual, the good, the right, the expedient—that the potential for error is minimized.

Lippmann saw his role in society as a practitioner of such discourse. He sought to bring about what he perceives as the necessary mode of thought in men's minds, hoping it would lead to appropriate actions, to what Aristotle would call good ends. *Real Advocacy Journalism*™ is defined as a form of journalistic writing that is factual, thorough, and unbiased, which not only analyzes but is advisory in nature. Either by direct assertion, or implication, this discourse puts forth and defends a position designed to inform, persuade, and/or move a targeted public to action. There is an active attempt even with expository information, on the part of the advocate journalist, to influence public opinion regarding the issue on which he/she is writing, the purpose of which is to arrive at the greatest good.

The political columnist/commentator, advocate journalist, must be analytical, judgmental, and prescriptive in his/her focus and approach. Such an approach embodies and uniquely combines elements of all aspects in order to provide audiences with the most complete, most comprehensive picture available on the subject matter under discussion.

This means that it is necessary for the political columnist/pundit/commentator, in the development of a position on any given issue, to construct a judicial element by urging that some assessment be made on the part of the listener or reader, of relevant past events in terms of their harmfulness, justness, or goodness. This is generally done, particularly in the case of Lippmann, by offering historical examples and other analogies from the past. Concomitantly, a judgment is being rendered, not only on that historical event, but also on the present state of affairs, or present act, deed, or condition, or whatever factors kindled the need for deliberation and decision to take place. And, of course, the deliberation is undertaken to point out the advantages and disadvantages of a course of action for the immediate as well as long-range future.

The genre of *Real Advocacy Journalism*™ is directed at two kinds of audiences—decision-makers, as well as spectators—instead of one or the other. Such discourse is directed to the decision-makers because they are the direct actors. They create. They determine. It is also directed to the spectators because they are the supportive bystanders. They are in a position to lend support, to align themselves with one side or the other, and therefore determine the outcome of a policy or course of action. Lippmann directed his books and commentary to both types of audiences.

While the basic characteristics of *Real Advocacy Journalism*™ are utilized in both Lippmann's books and newspaper column, one can observe how he adjusted the discourse in his column according to situational constraints, i.e., the nature and make-up of his newspaper audiences, and the nature of the newspaper as a medium which requires that one conforms to a certain style of writing, that one presents concepts in a more simplified form so that they may be easily grasped and readily understood; and of course, the constraint that one meets the ever-present time deadline for publication. Therefore, Lippmann's column is an abbreviated, more simplified version of the analysis and arguments he offers on a more elaborate, more complicated level in his books.

There are two other less tangible characteristics which seem to define *Real Advocacy Journalism*™ as a genre of discourse, and both characteristics are found in Lippmann's writings: A strong sense of authoritativeness, and a sense of an ultimate mission, a purpose for good that permeate the discourse.

Real Advocacy Journalism™ appears to be authoritative in nature in that one senses or is made to sense that the advocate journalist is an authority. There are reasons, whether the reasons can be articulated or not, for believing that the advocate journalist is trained, capable, and qualified to assess, to advise, to prescribe. The advocate journalist has been endowed, by experience, devoted study, a divine overseer, or any combination thereof to be about the business of enlightening and leading the masses, and the advocate journalist, therefore, warrants an attentive ear.

A sense of mission is also implied by the nature of *Real Advocacy Journalism*™. The advocate journalist is about the mission of leading mankind toward those means, those good ends, which will bring ultimate happiness, fulfillment, and the betterment of society. The advocate journalist, through his discourse, is to prevent a disastrous or catastrophic turn of events from occurring or certainly to warn of its imminence and prepare the public for its impact. In this regard one can detect a sense of urgency in its tone. *Real Advocacy Journalism*™ appears to be missionary in its vision, always striving for the best outcomes, the greater good.

This sense of mission is corroborated by other contemporary columnists/commentators of Lippmann as they expressed how they perceive their roles. Eric Sevareid, in his interview with the author, describes this sense of mission as an effort to "train" one's readers to think along the right lines, to elucidate an issue and advocate what position ought to be taken on that issue.[93] James Reston, in his interview with the author, says he feels compelled to write to his friend back home, "to make him aware of what is really going on" and to "inform him on some issue he is concerned about or ought to be concerned about."[89] Marquis Childs, in his interview with the author, describes it as an "addiction," one "feels compelled to shed as much light on the subject as possible if they feel they are at some vantage point."[90]

Lippmann used a variety of advocatory techniques in writing and publishing his columns as showed in the next chapter. In his books, he made extensive use of historical examples, historical analogies; he used both inductive and deductive reasoning in the construction of his logical arguments. He appealed to source credibility in reference to himself and others he considered authorities in a given issue area.

Lippmann is characterized as having been a very lucid writer, able to penetrate complex issues and make them simple and easy to understand. One explanation for his lucidity, and what may be characteristic of the ideal form of the genre, is the ability to label, to name, to define and redefine. Lippmann was also effective in constructing hypothetical examples.

In his columns, Lippmann's advocatory approach was different. He made more use of contemporaneous examples and analogies as opposed to historical ones. Elaborate or extended logical arguments were replaced by the use of enthymemes, maxims, and truisms.

For the purposes of demonstrating *Real Advocacy Journalism*™ in action, we will examine three issues that Lippmann repeatedly addressed in his books and put into practice as he covered related issues in his columns. Again, those three issues are: 1) the role of government; 2) the role of the public in shaping public policy; and 3) the role of the public philosophy in sustaining and fostering the good society. While the general purposes and positions regarding the three issues examined are basically the same in both Lippmann's books and newspaper columns, there are marked differences in advocatory techniques and styles, in how Lippmann treated or developed those issues in the respective situations for different audiences.

The advocatory techniques used in the books as opposed to the newspaper column varied in degree of complexity and level of abstractness. One reason for the variation in techniques is that the columns represented an abbreviated, ad hoc, more simplistic application of principles and theories developed in his books. However, such differences were also brought about because of the constraints of the medium of the newspaper mentioned earlier. For example, while a heavy reliance on history and the assessment of historical events appear to be a basic characteristic of *Real Advocacy Journalism*™, the extent of the analysis of historical events and the nature and type of historical example selected to illustrate a point differ in degree in Lippmann's books and his newspaper columns.

In his books, Lippmann relied heavily on elaborate historical analogies, historical references, and historical examples to support and illustrate his claims. Where there appeared that none were readily available for the point Lippmann wished to make, he constructed his own hypothetical examples and analogies based on related historical events. The historical analogies and examples used in Lippmann's columns were almost always simple in nature. If a historical reference was made, it was not usually one of obscurity, but rather one of either recent history or one of common familiarity.

Logical reasoning, particularly inductive reasoning, was also used extensively by Lippmann; elaborate arguments are developed in his books. The use of enthymemes, maxims, and truisms in his newspaper column replaced the use of extended logical reasoning or elaborate arguments used in his books. This is particularly true if the subject matter was not treated in a number of consecutive columns. For those issues to which Lippmann devoted several columns, one can see many of the advocatory techniques used in his books. Lippmann's treatment of the issue of the Cold War is an example. During the period of the Cold War, many of his columns addressed the issues involved in a sequential and serial fashion. The columns were later compiled and published in book form. And one can readily see his premises, his arguments, and his conclusion unfold in a well-developed coherent fashion.[91]

A dominant advocatory technique found more in Lippmann's newspaper column than in his books is a reliance on source credibility. Much of his newspaper discourse is characterized by pure assertion on his part. He simply declared what he thought was the case or should have been the case. If any support or evidence was offered, it came in the form of a reference to, or a quotation from what was considered a well-known authoritative source.

But what may be distinctive in Lippmann's discourse in terms of advocatory techniques, and, therefore, distinctive of the genre of *Real Advocacy Journalism*™, is his widespread and effective use of labels. He captured and conveyed ideas or concepts through discriminate naming and labeling.

Lippmann has also been described as having the ability to write "in language, which is precise enough for a Supreme Court Justice, simple enough for a ward-heeler and entertaining enough to woo a magnate from his grapefruit." With that description he was also saluted as "the man with the Flashlight

Mind, the Great Elucidator."[92] James Reston says of Lippmann: "He always had something to say. He had an unusual gift of cutting through the underbrush, and while he did not try to write in the vernacular—he rather deplored it—he used the English language as it should be used."[93]

Definitions, repetition of an idea at strategic intervals during a discursive piece, and the development of parallel ideas are distinctive techniques used by Lippmann. He also made excellent use of advocatory questions to guide his readers along the right train of thought. These techniques are found in both his books and his newspaper column.

In addition to his methods of establishing a position about an issue, what was Lippmann's advocatory style? Figurative language is a feature throughout Lippmann's work. Harold Laski, in a letter to a friend, said "I wish I had Lippmann's pen because he makes words talk to themselves."[94] His writing is characterized by both abstractness and concreteness as Lippmann offered both philosophical perspectives and practical solutions. One finds more abstract or philosophical ideas advanced in his books than in his column. His treatment of issues in his column stayed within the realm of the practical.

Lippmann almost always wrote in an eloquent and elevated style. Common parlance was rarely used in his books and only occasionally used in his columns. A patrician, aristocratic tone is a Lippmann trademark. Lippmann's use of language is both compelling and consuming as it evokes images, as it stirs, as it brings its pursuer to a state of belief. Sir Hubert Holmes, a peer of Lippmann, said: "He [Lippmann] is a born writer... his writing is fly paper for me—if I touch it, I am stuck till I finish it. There are few living I think who so discern and articulate the nuances of the human mind."[95] Harold Laski, in a similar vein, applauds the "sparse, nervous strength of his [Lippmann's] style that obviously reflects great mental power."[96]

Purpose and Role of the Practitioner of Real Advocacy Journalism™

Lippmann's advocatory techniques cannot be examined or assessed without noting what Lippmann sought to achieve in his audience, and who he perceived his audience as being. Elizabeth Midgley, Lippmann's personal assistant from 1961 until his retirement, said to the author during an interview that "Lippmann saw his role primarily as a shaper of public opinion and to indirectly influence policy and public course of action." According to Midgley, "he sometimes wrote his column primarily to those in power and in a decision-making position. At other times he wrote to mobilize the public to influence those in power." Midgley cites Lippmann's columns during the Vietnam War as an example. After trying unsuccessfully to directly influence the policy of the Johnson administration, he decided to change the approach in his column and mobilize public opinion regarding the war, hoping the public would apply pressure on Johnson. Midgley says that one could also say Lippmann's purpose in part was "to educate his audience." But she hastens to add that "mainly his purpose was to influence the course of events, by shaping their opinions with reference to events."[97]

James Reston concurs with Midgley. Reston says of Lippmann's purpose and role: "He was trying to influence policy. He was very confident that his gift of writing and thinking were persuasive enough, that they would arrest the attention of the policymaker.... His great achievement was that he compelled the attention of policymakers, people in Congress, leaders at home and abroad and so on, and made them grapple with his ideas.... He wanted to be judged on whether he was right or wrong. Whether the policies that he was proposing, as if he were Secretary of State, were the right policies." Reston further states that Lippmann operated on the presumption that he knew "what ought to be done."[98]

Marquis Childs also asserts that Lippmann's "ultimate design was to influence policy and shape opinion." And Childs adds that Lippmann "had a certain arrogance about his own influence, and justifiably."[99]

Eric Sevareid said Lippmann, like himself, had a two-fold purpose, to elucidate and to advocate. Sevareid observes: "In my own case I've always attempted a training [of my audience]. I always lean to the function of trying to elucidate or to advocate [a position]."[100]

Aside from these observations, Lippmann himself provided hints of what he was trying to achieve through his discourse. Back at Harvard he felt it was the responsibility of those with special ability to help their fellow men "understand and adjust to reality." He later wrote about the importance of bringing about "the revolution in men's minds." And even at the twilight of his career he felt that in a democracy where the consent of the governed is crucial, it was up to the political columnist/commentator, the advocate journalist, through *Real Advocacy Journalism*™, to tell or interpret what it is that the governed is to consent to.

Lippmann's Audiences As Illustrative of Those of Real Advocacy Journalism™

The question of who comprised Lippmann's actual audience was raised at several points during his career. The readers of his books are numbered in the hundreds of thousands, and the readers of his column in the millions.[101]

But to whom was Lippmann addressing his column? Who can be adjudged to be his audience based on the nature of his discourse? William Allen White, in a review of Lippmann's *Interpretations*: 1931-1932 (a compilation of the columns written during 1931 and 1932), concluded that Lippmann wrote for the policy makers of the country. He found that Lippmann appealed neither to the "moronic underworld" nor the "smart and sophisticated," but rather "to the nation's leaders in politics, business and opinions molding."[102]

David Weingast also claims that Lippmann does not direct his column to the masses. "The level of his writing and the ideas he advocated appeal to a minority of newspaper readers;" Weingast tested samples of Lippmann's column over a five-year period based on a formula given in Rudolph Flesch's *The Act of Plain Talk*. According to the scale for measuring the difficulty of reading matter, Lippmann's columns were rated as "fairly difficult." Furthermore, according to this measure, forty percent of American adults were able to understand Lippmann's column at the time the test was conducted, and twenty-four percent constituted a "typical" reader, i.e., audience. Lippmann's "level" of writing during that time was compared to that found in "quality" magazines.[103] For those who were close to Lippmann, he wrote for two audiences, the educated lay person, policy makers and leaders.[104] Marquis Childs observes that Lippmann's column was "a highly literate column...I would be skeptical about the number of regular readers outside an elite."[105]

Eric Sevareid believes that Lippmann's columns were addressed "to the people with a lot of information already. That's why maybe his audience was much more limited.... He assumed people had a lot of information and he took off from that point." Sevareid illustrates his proof: "Ray Clapper used to be a columnist here [Washington], a very good one, for many years. He always used to say that you should never underestimate the intelligence of your audience and never overestimate their information. I think Walter did overestimate the information, the background that most people forget."[106]

Reston makes a similar assessment of Lippmann's audience. He describes its composition from the days when Lippmann was on the staff of *The New Republic* to the time when Lippmann became a political columnist.

Reston describes his perception of Lippmann's audience during the different phases of his career:

> I think when he left the *New Republic* and he went to the *World*, I think he saw that as going to a larger audience composed of the elites of the great city of New York, university people, financial people, the leaders of what was then the great city of America. Then when the *World* folded, he had all kinds of different ideas about what he wanted to do, but he decided to go to the column because that gave him the nation or even a world audience—the same kind of people he was aiming at. He was aiming at the policy makers. He was aiming at the thinkers. The only difference when he went into the column was that it was picked up, of course all over the country. Instead of reaching merely the Harvards, the Yales, the Princetons, the Columbians, and so on he was reaching the thoughtful people, and he was reaching Washington every day; and he was reaching London and Paris and Berlin and Moscow and Tokyo.[107]

In summary, the column's actual reading audience has been estimated to range from as many as ten million readers in the earliest years to over forty million during the later years. Lippmann, apparently addressed, his column to the elites in society, the leaders, the decision- makers, the educated, the thoughtful, and those in the public who were paying attention.

5

SAMPLES OF REAL ADVOCACY JOURNALISM™ APPLIED TO PERSISTENT ISSUES

L ippmann maintained throughout his public career that the role of the public simply should be that of express-ing approval or disapproval, or of aligning itself with or against the actions of those entrusted with decision-making powers.

This chapter, while noting the consistency of meaning and positions of these issues in both Lippmann's books and news-paper columns, will deal with how *Real Advocacy Journalism*™ is practiced in his columns.

Issue I: The Role of the Public in the Affairs of Government

Today, with CNN, the BBC, FOX, and other cable news chan-nels that can cover and bring events into our homes via TV, or wherever we are through our smartphone, computer via the Internet, publics still are unable to have a front-row seat to all aspects of those events. We are made aware of them occurring or having occurred. But, unless we have or take the time to stay engaged as various aspects unfold, we are still left with a snapshot of the event albeit occurring in real time. Furthermore, it may be hours, days, months, even years before most of the facts and surrounding circumstances are known. This is particularly the case in the aftermath of catastrophic events such as mass shootings, airplane crashes, earthquakes, a tsunami. Even more time may lapse before there is any discussion about public policy steps to take to prevent, avoid, or better address such e occurrences in the.

There are some events that may render themselves more amenable to being more fully covered—but still not completely—as they unfold. That is the case with a royal wedding, a presidential inaugural, a sporting event. However, it is impossible to provide the public with a complete picture of the wars occurring in the Middle East, Africa, parts of Europe, and in other parts of the world. It is even more challenging to understand all the reasons fueling those wars, such as ethnic cleansing, religious wars, political and geographical power grabs, pro democracies, terrorism, and the wars against terrorism. The list goes on.

Lippmann reaches the conclusion that because of the nature of contemporary society, and the inability of the public to perform the function of government, its relationship to government should be external. The public should only align itself with or against what the leaders and experts of public affairs advise or propose.

How does Lippmann present this position in his newspaper column? There is a radical departure in approach from those used in his books, i.e., his longer works. Lippmann almost totally abandons any philosophical arguments, even in the longer columns. Instead of using historical examples and analogies, contemporaneous analogies and examples dominate. Such advocatory choices are wise selections on the part of Lippmann because they demand less of his newspaper audience in gaining an understanding or being able to visualize the premises he advances. The newspaper reader is not required to follow an intricate process of philosophical and logical reasoning as the readers of Lippmann's books are required to do.

An understanding of Lippmann's arguments on the part of the newspaper reader is not contingent upon a well-developed sense of command of history, philosophy, or logic. The language of the columns, while quite vivid, is not characterized by abstractness or ideological concepts. Lippmann also shows his mastery of capitalizing on the event of the hour to present some aspect of his philosophy to the general public that he spent years developing in his books. Let us examine Lippmann's column on the role of the public more closely.

On April 10, 1941, during the Roosevelt administration, Lippmann chose, as an illustration, apparently an innocuous un-newsworthy statement Eleanor Roosevelt had made in an interview a few days before regarding some industrial disputes. Mrs. Roosevelt simply said that she had personally studied two or three of the issues involved in the disputes in order to form a definite opinion. And she hoped that the general public would likewise suspend judgment until they had sufficiently studied the issues in each case. But in order that everyone might be informed, she suggested that local committees of private citizens be formed to report on the facts. In his "Today and Tomorrow" column on April 10, which he titled "Everybody's Business and Nobody's,"[1] Lippmann summarized what Mrs. Roosevelt had said and used it as the take-off point for the disquisition which followed on what the public's role should be in any issue.

In principle, Mrs. Roosevelt's idea sounds plausible, Lippmann acknowledges at the outset. But he proceeds to prove it is in fact unworkable by attacking the assumptions which underlie the idea: "There is the assumption that Mrs. Roosevelt, in the course of her very busy days, has in fact been able to

study two or three large industrial disputes, get to the bottom of
them and reach a sound judgment. There is the assumption that
the rest of the adult population can, will, and should attempt
to have definite opinions not only on Mrs. Roosevelt's two or
three cases, but on any number of other intricate controversies
as well. There is the assumption that the mass of these opinions
constitutes a verdict by 'public opinion' which in a democracy
is final and controlling."[2]

Such assumptions in appearance seem very democratic, but
in practice they undermine and destroy democratic government.
Instead of an elaborate argument, Lippmann states a maxim:
"When everyone is supposed to have a judgment about everything, nobody in fact is going to know much about anything."
Lippmann follows this maxim with an example, which raises
the question of whether Mrs. Roosevelt's study of the issue
was feasible or adequate, and she, more than likely, had more
time to devote than the average citizen. "If Mrs. Roosevelt...
knows the facts and has weighed the merits in two or three of
these recent industrial disputes, she has a capacity for rapid
investigation and quick analysis which not many of us possess."
For, "it took the mediation board, with all the experts of the
federal and state governments helping them twenty hours of
hard work to get to the bottom of the Allis-Chalmers affair; how
many private citizens in this country can give twenty minutes
to Allis-Chalmers, and another twenty minutes to Ford, and
another to Coal, and so on and so on?"[3]

From this, Lippmann reasons, using common parlance that
nothing is to be gained by trying to involve all the public. Chaos
is the inevitable result: "The only effect of inviting everybody
to judge every public question," says Lippmann, "is to confuse
everybody about everything." It is impossible 'for all people to
know all about all things, and the pretense that they can and
that they do is a bad illusion."

They neither have the time to study everything nor the competence to judge everything. Lippmann uses a readily understandable example, which his newspaper audience of that time could relate to in order to support his claim:

> The general public can judge whether employers and employees are cooperating, or are quarrelling, and it can demand that they find ways of cooperating. It can judge whether Secretary Perkins and the National Labor Relations Board and the Mediation Board are or are not achieving uninterrupted production. If they are not, the general public can insist that the President and Congress do something about it. But the general public cannot be the judge and the jury in each case. Nor can it decide just what specific measures the President and the Congress ought to adopt.[4]

Lippmann, using familiar references as opposed to historical ones, follows the example with a brief assessment on the qualification of the public: "The general public consists of men and women who read the newspapers and listen to the radio for a little time each day in the midst of busy lives. They can no more hope to have final opinions on every disputed question than they have opinions on what to do about pneumonia. All they can do about pneumonia is to get the best doctor they can find, and then call in another doctor if the first one does not seem to be satisfactory."[5]

In order to mitigate and counter possibly a negative response from his audience—with his claims of public ineptness which many of his readers could have found insulting or undemocratic—Lippmann cleverly shows how the public is short-changed when it assumes more in the decision-making process than was intended. He simultaneously reminds men in public affairs of the obligation and duty of their station. "But worse still," observes Lippmann, "this notion that everybody is to decide everything destroys the sense of responsibility in public men and deprives public opinion of responsible leadership. Effective government cannot be conducted by legislators and officials who, when a question is presented, ask themselves first and last, not what is the truth, and which is the right and necessary course but 'What does the Gallup poll say?' and 'How do the editors and commentators line up?'"[6]

It is not in the name of democracy that public men defer and evade their responsibilities by asking the mass of people to do the work they are supposed to do. Once public men refuse to lead opinion and choose to be led by it instead, it is impossible for sound public opinion to form. Lippmann once again illustrates with contemporaneous references:

> ...the President and the Administration Officials and the Congressmen in touch with them have the means for informing themselves on the realities for the labor situation and of the defense program and of the war that no one else, not even the most conscientious newspaper reporters, can possess. If with their responsibilities and their means of knowing what is what, they sit around waiting for the Gallup poll and the fan mail, they will get a Gallup poll and fan mail from a people that have not been able to know what men must know in order to judge wisely—that is, to face their responsibility and to decide questions by consulting other responsible men and then to explain their decision, leaving to the people to judge whether the decision is reasonable and the results good.[7]

To convey to his newspaper audience how the complexity of contemporary society has made it virtually impossible for the public to have more than an external role in the execution of public affairs, Lippmann uses the commonplace easily understandable analogy of the town hall meeting instead of the concept of the pseudo-environment which he develops and refers to in most of his books:

> It is possible to run the affairs of a village by a town meeting. But the methods of the town meeting will not regulate the affairs of a great republic, which embraces a continent which is depending upon a hemisphere and is involved in one of the great crises of history. What is a virtue in a town meeting—to let everyone decide everything—becomes in the conduct of a great government the vice of responsibility, indecision, demagogy, and moral timidity. Mrs. Roosevelt cannot weigh and judge every industrial dispute and the rest of us certainly cannot. All we can do is to uphold the hands of, and then hold responsible for the results, those entrusted with the task of maintaining industrial peace.[8]

Following this analogy, Lippmann seeks to move the audience toward the premise that this principle of public alignment applies across the board to most of the difficult questions which confront the democracy. In the example which he offers as support, he invokes his own credibility as an element of proof:

> We have...the problem of the blockade and the feeding of various countries in Europe and northern Africa, and the country today is full of, argumentative committees and sincere men and women who think they know enough to know what should be done. I do not know

why they think they know enough. For having studied most of the information which is publicly available and talked with a great many more people who have some first-hand knowledge of the facts, all I know is that I do not know enough to have an opinion. All I know is that this infinitely complicated question will have to be decided by Mr. Churchill and the British government and Mr. Roosevelt and the really informed officials of the American government, and whether their decisions are wise or unwise, it is certain that I do not know enough to decide it for them.[9]

In this example, while showing that the public is ill-equipped to handle most difficult problems and issues, Lippmann established a common identity with the general public: He, even with his experience, is ill-equipped to handle some things.

Lippmann offers yet another example, involving a contemporaneous event as opposed to a historical one, of the public functioning only in a supportive role:

The same principle applies to the question of delivering the goods of the Allies under the lease-lend program. The decision as to how that can best be done is one that must be made by the President in consultation with his advisors and with other responsible public men. How is the outside public to know what "convoying" involves and whether it is the best system of protecting cargoes when, as a matter of fact, there is a respectable body of expert opinion which thinks there is a better system of protecting cargoes?

The question is not one which can be solved for the President by public debate. For the public cannot possibly foresee the consequences of doing certain things.[10]

And Lippmann concludes:

It is the President's responsibility, of which he cannot divest himself, to judge as wisely as he can what in the end is likely to be the right course, to make that judgment on the best advice he can obtain, to explain his decision and then trust that the people will support a conscientious, carefully considered decision.[11]

So, we see in Lippmann's column an exposition and advocacy of the same ideas regarding the role of the public and public opinion he advances in his books. What changes is his method of presenting those ideas in the two different advocatory situations. One is a more simplified version of the other.

The difference in advocatory style and techniques found in Lippmann's books and columns is testimony of his excellent adaptation of his discourse to very different audiences. While his books seem to be written more for the steady student of politics and philosophy with the many historical analogies, abstract conceptualizations, and logical arguments which characterized them, his columns seem to be written for the political actors—the everyday decision-makers and spectators of public affairs. Advocatory techniques were characterized by more simple analogies of contemporary events, familiar and common historical references, and non-technical, non-abstract concepts and language. Where the reader might find it necessary to digest slowly the discourse in Lippmann's books to grasp its meaningfulness, because of its technical and philosophical emphasis, the reader of Lippmann's column can gather the meaning rather readily.

This characterization of advocatory techniques is true of Lippmann's discourse as he advised on many subjects in both the philosophical realm of books and the practical realm of the newspaper column. This is also seen to be consistent as we examine Lippmann's purpose, form, and advocatory techniques in his practice of *Real Advocacy Journalism*™. This becomes evident as we examine another issue Lippmann dealt with over time: the role of government in contemporary society. Again, we see consistency of purpose, form, and advocatory technique in both his books and his columns, respectively.

What is profound in Lippmann's position on the role of the public in the affairs of government are the implications for politicians, for elected officials, and others working in government. First and foremost, they have the responsibility for ensuring that government makes the right decision and advances the right paths for the greater good of the entity and its citizens. Politicians, and those in powerful positions, should not rely on, fall victim to, take actions, or fail to take actions based upon the opinion of the public. Lippmann decries the use of polls by politicians, which has become commonplace in today's political environment to determine and dictate their actions, rather than pursuing the right and best course of action.

Lippmann is clearly urging advocate journalists, pundits, and politicians to not abdicate their role and responsibility of consulting the experts, availing themselves of the most pertinent and critical information, and arrive at the best solutions. Only then should they go before the public, explain their decision, and ask for consent or rejection. That is what constitutes the appropriate relationship between the public and the affairs of government.

Issue II: The Role of Government in Promoting the Good Society

Lippmann perceived government as having two primary roles, that of protector and provider. Besides protecting the state from any foreign invasions, government should serve as the ombudsman of individual rights by controlling the tendency toward evilness, selfishness, exploitation, and greed found in man as he engages in business and social transactions with his fellow man. As provider, government is to deliver those services necessary for the general well-being of the public and the overall maintenance of the state that the people either as individuals or groups cannot deliver. One can observe a shift in emphasis regarding the two functions of government at different stages of Lippmann's career, but the two premises of government's role as protector and provider remained consistent.

Lippmann also had ideas as to how these two primary functions could be accomplished. The state must perform its protective functions without becoming an "exalted policeman," an "agent of repression," and it must provide needed services and safeguards without stripping the individual of self-reliance and self-determination.

Lippmann shows that the concept of the state functioning as an exalted policeman is an inadequate and ineffective one. How did he deal with the inadequacies of this misconception of government in his column?

Lippmann makes an interesting, but effective, transition in treating the issue in his column. The whole idea of government is translated into a common concept, an easily recognizable and comprehensible symbol—"law and order." Lippmann shows how government fails to address the real needs of its citizens when it chooses to police their moral conduct. And, how in the end, such attempts are futile. Observe Lippmann's approach in a column he wrote for *Metropolitan*, in 1915. It is labeled simply, "Law and Order":

> Our statute books are cluttered with legislation that represents somebody's good intention, rather than a real insight into what is possible. And these laws cannot be enforced in a country where the sense of democracy is

strong. The law, to be more than a sham, must represent the real desire to obtain the consent of the biggest portion of the community. It does no good to legislate a morality which only the angels practice; it does only harm to pass bills which run counter to the deepest tendencies of the age. Yet many of our laws about sex and about business are so utterly unrelated to the ordinary lives of the American people that breaking the law is almost a national habit.

In this column, Lippmann also advances his belief that government should be continuously about the business of enacting laws that make the conditions of life better, not just about the business of policing morals:

This lawlessness will continue until we make up our minds that legislation in a democracy is, first of all, a series of common rules which enables us to live together without too much friction; then, that law is a way of spending money for our cities and countryside so that we shall all have a better chance to live. Law is not a method of making us perfect. Perfection cannot be legislated at Albany or Washington. Neither is it a method of strangling everything that is new, and of putting a damper on all aspirations. In order to be effective, law in a democracy must be elastic, not brittle; it must be capable of changing and adapting itself to growth; it must set no impossible ideals; it must be satisfied at any particular moment with the best that is possible under the circumstances. So far as morals go, the law is concerned with the minimum. It sets the standard below which civilization should not sink, but it cannot pretend to say how the best of men should live.[12]

How does Lippmann deal with the concept of government providing the standard of life rather than functioning as a policeman in his column? In terms of style, form, and technique, Lippmann's discourse regarding this issue is consistent. Observe how Lippmann presents the case of why laissez-faire, as it was understood before the two world wars, can no longer exist. He carefully develops why government must assume the role of provider. He does it without even raising the phrase laissez-faire. He takes off on a contemporaneous event with which his audience could identify. His historical references are of recent history, ones which his audience either had directly experienced or had a vague memory of or an association with.

"The Dream of a Troubled Spirit," appeared in the "Today and Tomorrow" column on January 20, 1949. Excerpts of the column are presented not only to show the consistency in Lippmann's form, style, and technique but also to show how he successfully translates and relates complicated economic ideas to understandable concepts, how he leads his readers to a state of understanding by putting events and the actions of certain key and visible actors of the day into perspective.

Lippmann connects the reader to a contemporaneous historical event—The New Deal. He elaborates:

> The sovereign idea of what became known as the New Deal is that the government is charged with the responsibility for the successful operation of the economic order and the maintenance and improvement of the standard of life for all classes in the nation. Though one could find an anticipation of his revolutionary idea in the Square Deal of President Theodore Roosevelt and in the New Freedom of President Woodrow Wilson, it was not until the great depression during the Hoover Administration that it became the established American doctrine.

Through historical references, Lippmann explains by implication not only when the principle of laissez-faire worked but
how it worked:

> It would never have occurred to Grant in 1873 or to
> Cleveland in 1893 or to Harding in 1912 that the federal
> government could or should, tell farmers, bankers, busi-
> nessmen, debtors and creditors, employers and employees
> what to do to restore prosperity, or that public officials
> had the right to use all the powers of the government
> and to draw upon all the national resources to protect
> the standard of life. Until the Hoover Administration
> the business cycle was supposed to be like the seasons
> and the weather, something you talked about but did
> nothing about while the unemployed walked the streets,
> the insolvent debtors were foreclosed, the bankrupt went
> bankrupt, and nature took its course.

Lippmann, still developing his case, and leading his reader to
a state of understanding, uses a recent historical event to explain
when laissez-faire ceased to be viable and why government had
to change its course:

> On August 11, 1932, President Hoover made an address,
> accepting the Republican nomination, which is certainly
> one of the most important, as it is one of the most
> neglected, public documents of this century. He declared
> that when "the forces of destruction"—that is to say, the
> great depression—invaded the American economy and
> brought about "bank and business failures, demoraliza-
> tion of security and real property values, commodity
> prices and unemployment...two courses were open. We
> might have done nothing. That would have been utter

ruin. Instead, we met the situation with proposals to private business and the Congress of the most gigantic program of economic defense and counterattack ever evolved in the history of the Republic."

And, so, we have the new imperative placed on government:

Mr. Hoover, in language that was then unprecedented, declared that "the function of the federal government in these times is to use its reserve powers and its strength for the protection of citizens and local governments by support to our institutions against forces beyond their control." That was the commitment born of dire necessity and of hope, by which government is held responsible in respect to the standard of life of the people. No one since then who was President, or sought to be, has ever challenged or renounced this commitment.[13]

Lippmann repeatedly treated the role of government as provider in a number of his columns throughout the years. His advocatory method remains consistent. In 1958, for example, in a column entitled "Crucial Internal Questions," he begins simply:

In its essence, the question is whether the United States can afford to do the things which it needs to do. Can it afford to run successfully in the race of armaments? And can it also afford a foreign policy which sustains our alliances and helps to finance the undeveloped countries? And can it also pay for the schools, hospitals, roads, airports, the reclamation and the conservation and the other public services and facilities which our rapidly expanding urbanized population requires? And can it also make it possible for the people as private individuals to raise their personal standards of life?[14]

He takes contemporaneous events and explains and advises with regards to his position.

Again in 1960, in a column entitled "The Size of the Problem," he says:

Here at home the overriding question is how to pay for the public needs of our growing population in an era when our social order is relentlessly challenged. These public needs include not only the rising costs of the race of armaments and the competition among the under-developed nations. They include also the rising costs of scientific research, of better public schools, of more adequate hospitals and public health services, public works, roads, water supply and sewage disposal, slum clearance and urban renewal.[15]

The pattern of development was the same.

There were many other columns devoted to the question of what the role of government should entail. Such columns addressed both functions as Lippmann saw them. Columns such as: "Regulating the Labor Unions," "On the Grandchildren's Future," "Fact Finding and Steel," "The School Crisis," and "Polio Vaccine and Public Policy," are representative examples of how Lippmann dealt with the role of government in his column.[16]

In addressing the role of government in promoting the good society, Lippmann is most directly speaking to politicians and those that the public has entrusted to thoroughly immerse themselves in the myriad of issues that government confronts and must put laws and policies in place to address them adequately and effectively. They must endeavor to put forth to the public the best solutions based upon the purpose and capacity of government. They owe those who elected them nothing less. Politicians should never subjugate or supplant this obligation to self-interests, or undue influence of special interest groups. The public interest should always prevail in caring out the affairs of government. That is the politician's calling.

Issue III: Critical Role of the Public Philosophy

Lippmann's treatment of the role of the public philosophy or the traditions of civility (he uses the phrases interchangeably) can be considered as the ultimate argument advanced during his career. The public philosophy is presented as the missing link through which, when found and put in its proper place, man will be able not only to work towards, but perhaps finally achieve the good society. It is certain, however, in Lippmann's eyes, if the public philosophy is not revered and reviewed, societal doom is certain.

It is in Lippmann's treatment of the public philosophy that we find his most complex, most philosophically oriented arguments. He is unmistakably a Platonist in much of his appeal. The influence of the idea of "realm of spiritual essence" which his teacher, philosopher George Santayana, espoused is pervasive.

The form, style, and advocatory techniques of Lippmann's discourse are once again consistent in nature and the pattern is clear. He makes use of elaborate historical analogies and examples, along with well-developed logical arguments to present a persuasive case in his books. In his column, while the purposes and positions are consistent with those in his books, his advocatory techniques and style of language are more simplified. He makes use of contemporaneous events for analysis. His historical references are simpler and more familiar (usually of recent history as opposed to distant history), and truism or enthymemes have replaced the elaborate logical reasoning.

How does Lippmann present the role of the public philosophy in his columns? In his columns, was he able to effectively articulate the abstract notion of the public philosophy and its critical role in society and social cohesion? Again, Lippmann's form, style, and advocatory techniques are consistent with the established pattern. He capitalizes on a current event and attempts to explain the working of the public philosophy in society. In a column dealing with the coronation of Queen Elizabeth IV in 1953, the public philosophy has been described as "common center of allegiance." Lippmann begins:

> Many men who live far beyond the Commonwealth and Empire have come to feel, as the coronation of the Queen drew near, that though they have no part in the gorgeous ceremony, they do participate in the solemn rite. For the British have made out of the forms and usages of their own unique history a great work, which celebrates the saving truth about the government of men.

Lippmann through the effective technique of renaming proceeds to translate the "traditions of civility" into "a common center of allegiance." Note the contrast the two labels present. But they both describe the public philosophy and its purpose:

> It is the truth that in every good society there must be a common center, known to be legitimate, to which the loyalty and the public love of all men are bound. That center of allegiance may be incarnate in an actual person or, as in a republic, it may be disembodied and have its being in the idea of the constitution and its ideal meaning. But always and everywhere, if a government is to be

good, a center of men's allegiance must be recognized that is above the diversities and conflicts of their interests, and that is invulnerable to the pressure of party, faction, class, race, and sect. And since this center of men's worldly allegiance must be beyond the reach of their worldly passions, it must be founded in, it must be consecrated to, the realm of the spirit. It must be bound to the truths that are more than the private and passing opinions of persons and of crowds, and to the laws that are above their wishes and their impulses.

Lippmann goes on to explain how the coronation of the queen not only symbolizes but embodies the public philosophy and perpetuates its fervor in the minds of men.

This is the universal essence which Queen Elizabeth II represents for all mankind when she is recognized, is sworn, is anointed, and is crowned. In the corners of the centuries, the British people—the most gifted in government since the Romans and with their genius in poetry—have invested monarchy with the meaning that must be recognized somewhere and somehow in any state whether or not it has a king, if it is to be governed well.

The ritual itself is an eloquent record of how this has been done, so often against the will of the reigning monarch himself. The ritual looks back upon and sums up the centuries of struggle and of inspiration in which the British have brought all earthly powers—kings, nobles, and all the commoners no less—under the laws. It is a great art to have woven about their hereditary and not always very royal and admirable kings, a web of usages and symbols and ceremonies which—though they are

unique for the British people in their concrete and historical circumstance—are none the less true and significant
for all peoples and all states.

Lippmann concludes by emphasizing the timeliness of the
event, more importantly the timeliness of the ideas and truths
it represents. For there is an urgent need for contemporary
democracy to make contact with these truths:

> The truths of this rite are most timely for our day. Our
> generation would, in any circumstances, be more sensi-
> tive and receptive to them than those that have preceded
> us, even if by great good fortune the central figure were
> not the young and beautiful Queen attended by her
> great Prime Minister, so undoubtedly the chivalrous and
> dauntless champion of freedom and good hope. This is a
> moment to reaffirm and to celebrate the essential truths.
> For the future of the free democratic societies hangs in
> the balance because, confronted with the challenge of
> their adversaries, they are so weakened by the conflict
> and confusion within and among themselves.
>
> If the free world is in this great peril, it is not because
> the adversaries of freedom are so strong or so attractive
> but because so many, indeed most, of the large demo-
> cratic states are at the moment so badly governed. In
> many of them, our own also included, good government
> is undermined by the usurpation of the sovereign power
> by the popular assembly. In the crisis of our Western
> society this usurpation has brought about a paralysis and
> of the whole free world, and to destroy the freedom and
> kindly community of men with one another at home.[17]

Writing a year later and using another contemporaneous event to illustrate a philosophical position, Lippmann addressed the importance of the tradition of civility being consciously recognized as the threads of fabric which holds the good society together. In this particular instance he was attending the state opening of parliament and the tribute to Prime Minister Winston Churchill in Westminster Hall. In this column which he entitled "The Bonds of Affection" Lippmann has labeled or defined the public philosophy as "a loyalty to the enduring nation."

Lippmann begins his column with a description of the event:

> A few years ago, I would have felt differently than I did last Tuesday morning in London when I had the good luck to see the state opening of Parliament and the tribute to Churchill in Westminster Hall. Anyone at any time would be fascinated by the splendor and brilliance of the ceremony in the House of Lords, and deeply moved by seeing full justice done publicly to the great man. But for an American today there was also, I could not help feeling, a poignant reminder that something at home, which is infinitely precious, is in danger of being lost.

What is this something that is so well represented in parliament, but is on the eve of being lost in America? Lippmann says:

> That something is a loyalty to the enduring nation which is so compelling that it keeps party politics, and the competition for votes and for popular applause, in their proper place. That proper place is well below, and far apart from, the high concerns of the state in its dealings abroad and, at home, in the administration of justice. Churchill, in his speech replying to Mr. Attlee, spoke of "that characteristic British parliamentary principle

cherished in both Lords and Commons, don't bring politics into private life." The principle, so an American can
feel, is broader than that. It is not to let politics invade
every nook and cranny of public life until the whole
institutional framework of the nation is submerged and
overwhelmed by ambitious and quarrelling men.[18]

Lippmann puts his readers in touch with their history by
offering this comparison:

> We have begun to realize in these days how close we have
> come to separating the coming generation from its heri-
> tage in the American past; we are shocked and dismayed
> to discover how unreal the great Americans have become
> to them, how the events which have formed the nation
> are dim, how dangerously close we have come to being
> a people who inhabit the land with their bodies without
> possessing it in their souls.
>
> But we must know also that there is no short way to
> make the past live again in men's minds; it cannot be
> done by passing a law, or by appropriating money, or by
> a witch hunt among the professors. The American past
> can be brought to life again only by men who tell the
> majestic story once more, aware that they are making
> history and not merely writing it. When we read the
> writings of the early Americans, we find that, unlike
> our own generation, the past was continually present in
> their minds as part of their own experience. They were
> making a new government, and for their own guidance,
> for knowledge of what to do, they drew not upon surveys
> of contemporary opinion and questionnaires but upon
> precedence and experience.[19]

The remainder of the column is written in excellent form, using vivid moments in history to illustrate the necessity of keeping the tradition alive. Much of this column is so applicable to the political environment in which we find ourselves today.

Again, writing in May of 1940 on the eve of America entering her Second World War, Lippmann lamented:

> The tragic ordeal through which the Western world is passing was prepared in the long period of easy liberty during which men forgot the elementary truths of human existence.... They forgot that unless they bear themselves so that the eternal values of truth, justice and righteousness are perpetually revealed to them, they will not know how to resist the corrosion of their virtue or how to face the trials that life will bring to them upon this earth. They had become too comfortable and too safe and too sophisticated to believe the first things and the last things which men have been inspired to understand through generations of suffering, and they thought it clever to be cynical, and enlightened to be unbelieving, and sensible to be soft.
>
> And so, through suffering, they must rediscover these first and last things again, and be purified once more by repentance.
>
> The free peoples of the Western world have lived upon a great inheritance which they have squandered recklessly. When they were put to the test, they had come to the point where they took the blessings of this inheritance so totally for granted that they no longer knew, and their schools had almost ceased to teach them, and their leaders were afraid to remind them, how the laws and the institutions and the great controlling customs of our civilization were made. They thought that the God

whom they believed in dimly or not at all had conferred these blessings upon them gratuitously, that somehow they, as distinguished from their own ancestors and from millions of their fellow beings in less fortunate lands, were exempt from the labors and the sacrifices and the trials of man. They did not know that the products of civilization which they so greedily consumed are not the enduring inheritance of man....

What is left of our civilization will not be maintained, what has been wrecked will not be restored, by imagining that some new political gadget can be invented, some new political formula impoverished which will save it. Our civilization can be maintained and restored only by remembering and rediscovering the truths, and by re-establishing the virtuous habits on which it was founded. There is no use looking into the blank future for some new and fancy revelation of what man needs in order to live....[20]

While written in 1940, Lippmann could have just as easily have written it today, given the political circumstances in which we find ourselves in 2021, some eighty years after this column was originally written.

Philosophically, Lippmann has come full circle in advancing the renewal of the public philosophy. The answer to contemporary man's problem lies in him making contact with an intangible concept which says there is something above his personal desires, his passions, his interests, his day-to-day survival, even something above governments and kings to which he owes ultimate allegiance. This higher law is the one and only all-controlling factor. Allegiance to it will not only dictate contemporary man's business and social conduct with his fellow man, but it will guide nations in their daily conduct of business. It has the potential of averting unnecessary wars and other destructive behaviors. Adherence to its principles is the only way civilization can continue to survive.

How will the public philosophy be revived? Who is to rid the public of its agnosticism? Men/women of "light and leading," proclaims Lippmann. The philosophers, the public educators, the advocate journalists, other pundits, and politicians—they are to transmit the traditions of civility through their teachings, their writings, their policies, and practices from generation to generation. They, the persuader of publics, the men/women of "light and leading," must keep the traditions of civility alive in men's souls, in their minds. To rely on the men/women of "light and leading" to cultivate our minds and thought is comparable to relying on the experts to determine the proper course in practical problems.

While Lippmann recognizes the problems men/women of "light and leading" may face in trying to make the intangible concept of the public philosophy viable to contemporary man, he does not offer a static prescription about how it can be accomplished. He acknowledges that the proof of viability of the public philosophy must be compelling, if man is to regain faith. But it is not to be done by exhortation nor by a rereading of the classics. Then one begs to ask, what will make the public philosophy compelling to contemporary man? Making it relevant and relatable in how it can address and minimize the ever-present forces that are always at work to marginalize and subjugate the best interest of the good society to that of despots and the selfish interest of the few.

We have seen Lippmann address himself to three major issues continuously impacting contemporary man. He has addressed the role of public opinion in the governmental process today. He has grappled with what should be the role of government in society; and he has dealt with the ultimate question of survival by dealing with the notion that the public needs to recapture the public philosophy, the tradition of civility to promote the greatest good for the greatest number.

In one of the final interviews Lippmann granted before his death, he spoke of the problem of survival. The interviewer observed: "You Mr. Lippmann are really one of the few columnists, perhaps the last one, who has a philosophy, who tries to see the world in a specific perspective and who tries to analyze events as they fit your own philosophy." Lippmann responded: "If I am perhaps the last it is because there is no available philosophy around that fits the revolutionary period in which we live." Lippmann continued: "This is not the first time that human affairs have been chaotic and seemed ungovernable. But never before, I think, have the stakes been so high. I am not talking about, nor do I expect a catastrophe like nuclear war. What is really pressing upon us is that the number of people who need to be governed and those who are involved in governing threaten to exceed man's capacity to govern. This furious multiplication of the masses of mankind coincides with the ever more imminent threat that because we are so ungoverned, we are polluting and destroying the environment in which the human race must live."

The interviewer promptly asked: "Where does this lead us?" Lippmann replied: "The supreme question before mankind—to which I shall not live to know the answer—is how men will be able to make themselves."[21]

Lippmann died before completing his final book which was entitled *The Un-governability of Man*.[22] His concern about man, government, and the overall well-being of society was continuous. It was a pre-occupation during his tenure as a political columnist.

6

WHAT REAL ADVOCACY JOURNALISM™ REQUIRES OF THE PRACTITIONER

We have seen the consistency of positions and approaches Lippmann used in influencing publics. These theoretical underpinnings and their practical application have resulted in Lippmann codifying the genre of *Real Advocacy Journalism™*, and the crucial role it plays in contemporary society when correctly and consistently executed.

As a practicing political columnist, concerned with influencing public opinion and shaping public policy, Lippmann had overriding concepts and basic beliefs about what the role of the persuader of publics, particularly the advocate journalist, should be; what basic functions he/she is to perform in the process of enlightening the public and effectuating public opinion and public action on key issues.

Why did Lippmann choose the advocatory techniques of naming, labeling, redefining, historical analogies, analysis of contemporaneous events, and logical reasoning? Lippmann saw the political columnist/commentator, the advocate journalist, as needing three primary skills in carrying out his/her functions or purposes. In an attempt to perform the task of persuading a public, the advocate journalist should be able to: (1) separate words and their meanings and "disentangle" ideas; (2) be an effective "visualizer"—be able to create accurate representations of ideas or matters that are ordinarily invisible to contemporary man or normally out of his reach; and (3) have a good under-standing of the traits and characteristics of the target audience.

According to Lippmann, the first required skill of the advo-cate journalist is to be able to separate words and pinpoint their relevant meaning because the same word will connote any number of ideas to a group of people. Emotions are often displaced from the images to which they belong to names which resemble the names of these images. "On many subjects of great public importance" says Lippmann, "and in varying degree among different people for more personal matters, the threads of memory and emotion are in a snarl.... In the un-criticized parts of the mind there is a vast amount of association...."[1]

If the political columnist/commentator during the process of persuasion would engage in clarification, naming, enlight-enment, and re-education of this kind, it will help "to bring our public opinions into grip with the environment. That is the way the enormous censoring, stereotyping and dramatiz-ing apparatus can be liquidated. Where there is no difficulty in knowing what the relevant environment is, the critic, the teacher, the physician, [political columnists/commentators] can unravel the mind."[2]

Lippmann warns, however, that in cases where the environ-ment is as obscure to the political columnist, advocate journalist, as to the audience, no analytical technique is sufficient within itself to disentangle an idea to discover or an identifiable name. Lippmann says this is where our contemporary means for secur-ing the truth or knowledge come into play. In situations where the environment is unknown or obscure to the advocate journal-ist, intelligence work in the form of information gathering from the experts is required. "In political and industrial problems, for example, the critic as such can do something, but unless he can count upon receiving the expert reporter's valid picture of the environment, his dialectic cannot go far."[3] His disentangling and naming processes are hampered and limited.

Implicit in all of this, is that the advocate journalist should be about the business of determining the meaning of words[4] and disentangling ideas[5] for others in order that they may perceive, categorize, name their environment accurately and therefore act accordingly and appropriately.

The second required skill of a practitioner of *Real Advocacy Journalism*™ is to act as visualizer, to be able to capture and convey accurately and vividly those ideas, events, and matters which are ordinarily invisible to contemporary man, or normally beyond his reach or out of his realm of immediate consciousness. The advocate journalist is to wet his readers'/listeners' appetites, stimulate their creative and artistic faculties—all in an effort to accomplish within the reader/listener a more complete understanding, and therefore a fuller experience in the communication act. In other words, the advocate journalist is to act as visualizer in order to bring about the greatest degree of identification. And this is done by trying to involve and stimulate as much of the reader's/auditor's total consciousness as possible.

Lippmann says, "when public affairs are popularized in speeches, headlines, plays, moving pictures, cartoons, novels, statues or paintings, their transformation into a human interest requires first abstraction from the original, and then animation of what has been abstracted."[6] It is given that people are not generally interested in, or very moved by the things they do not see. And, of public affairs, the vast majority of people sees very little. Therefore, public affairs generally "remain dull and unappetizing until somebody with the makings of an artist, has translated them into a moving picture."[7]

When this occurs, "the abstraction, imposed upon our knowledge of reality by all the limitations of our access and of our prejudices, is compensated. Not being omnipresent and omniscient, we cannot see much of what we have to think and talk about. Being flesh and blood we will not feed on works and names and gray theory. Being artists of a sort, we paint pictures, stage dramas, and draw cartoons out of the abstractions."[8]

It is better, Lippmann readily acknowledges, if we can find "gifted men who can visualize for us." For all people do not find the time nor are they "endowed to the same degree with the pictorial faculty."[9] Lippmann was also aware that the mere visualizer has been accused of being too external, too cinematographic when it comes to presenting a phenomenon and less sensitive to the internal make-up of that phenomenon. Lippmann says, "For the people who have intuition, often appreciate the quality of an event and the inwardness of an act far better than a visualizer. They have more understanding when the crucial element is a desire that is never crudely overt, and appears on the surface only in veiled gesture, or in rhyme of speech. Visualization may catch the stimulus and the result. But the intermediate and internal is often as badly caricatured by a visualizer, as is the intension of the composer by an enormous soprano in the sweet maiden's part."[10]

Nevertheless, Lippmann hastens to add, "Though they often have as peculiar justice, intuitions remain highly private and largely incommunicable. But social intercourse depends on communication and while a person can often steer his own life with the utmost grace by virtue of his intuitions, he usually has great difficulty in making them real to others." When a person talks about intuitions, they sound like a "sheaf or mist." While intuitions give a fairer perception of human feelings "the reason with its spatial and tactile prejudice can do little with that perception."[11]

Lippmann concludes, "where action depends on whether a number of people are of one mind, it is probably true that in the first instance no idea is lucid for practical decision until it has visual or tactile value. But it is also true that no visual idea is significant to us until it has enveloped some stress of our own personality. Until it releases or resists, depresses or enhances, some craving of our own, it remains one of the objects which do not matter."[12]

The logical extension of Lippmann's theory of the visualizer being able to create the right picture or perspective, of course, is that pictures themselves will always be the surest way of conveying an idea. But next in order are words. They not only stimulate pictures in our memory, but they can also create mental pictures. It must be remembered that the idea conveyed is not fully the listener's or reader's own until he/she has identified himself/herself with some aspect of the picture.

So, one of the ultimate aims of the visualizer is to bring about identification within the listener or reader. "The identification," says Lippmann, "may be almost infinitely subtle and symbolic. The mimicry may be performed without our being aware of it, and sometimes in a way that would horrify those sections of our personality which support our self-respect. In sophisticated people the participation may not be in the fate of the hero, but on the fate of the whole idea to which both hero and villain are essential. But these are refinement."[13] Ordinarily, "in popular representation, the handles for identifications are almost always marked. One knows who the hero is at once. And no work of art promises to be easily popular where the marking is not definite and the choice clear."

According to Lippmann, that is not enough: "the audience must have something to do, and the contemplation of the true, the good and the beautiful is not something to do. In order not to sit inertly in the presence of the picture, and this applies as much to newspaper stories, as to fiction and the cinema, the audience must be exercised by the image."[14]

For illustrative purposes, Lippmann explains there are two forms of acts/behaviors, which far transcend all others in terms of ease with which they are aroused and eagerness with which stimuli for them are wrought.[15] Those acts/behaviors are sexual passion and fighting. They "have so many associations with each other, and they blend into each other so intimately," says Lippmann, "that a fight about sex outranks every other theme in the breadth of its appeal. There is none so engrossing or so careless of all distinctions of culture and frontiers."[16]

The sexual motif figures very little in American political imagery. But the fighting motif appears quite frequently. Politics is interesting when there is a fight or, as is often said, an issue. Often, in order to make politics popular or interesting, issues or fights have been created when there were none—none in the sense that the differences of judgment, or principle, or fact between the opposing camps do not call for the enlistment of aggressive or belligerent behavior among observers.[17] "Where pugnacity is not enlisted," asserts Lippmann, "those of us who are not directly involved find it hard to keep up our interest. For those who are involved, the absorption may be real enough to hold them even when no issue is involved. They may be exercised by sheer joy in activity, or by subtle rivalry or invention. But for those to whom the whole problem is external and distant, these other faculties do not easily come into play. In order that the faint image of the affair shall mean something to them, they must be allowed to exercise the love of struggle, suspense, and victory."[18]

In essence what Lippmann says to the advocate journalist, the practitioner of *Real Advocacy Journalism*™, is that a distant situation should not appear as a "gray flicker on the edge of attention." Rather it should be translated through words and

imagery into pictures in which the opportunity for strong identification is very recognizable. Unless this happens during the
communication process, events and issues will interest only a
few for a little while. Such issues "will belong to the sights seen
but not felt, to the sensations that beat on our sense organs,
and are not acknowledged." As observers, "we have to take
sides," says Lippmann. "We have to be able to take sides. In the
recesses of our being, we must step out of the audience on to
the stage, and wrestle as the hero for the victory of good over
evil. We must breathe into the allegory the breath of our life."[19]

The advocate journalist, political columnist/commentator,
as visualizer would do well to remember that the human mind
is not "a film which registers once and for all each impression
that comes through its shutters and lenses." It is endlessly and
persistently creative. "The pictures fade or combine, are shaped
here, condensed there as we make them more completely our
own. They do not lie inert upon the surface of the mind but are
reworked by the poetic faculty into a personal expression of ourselves. We distribute the emphasis and participate in the action."[20]

According to Lippmann, in order to become this personally
engaged, we personalize quantities and dramatize relations.
The affairs of the world are often represented as some sort of
allegory. For example, "Social Movements, Economic Forces,
National Interests, Public Opinion are treated as persons, and
persons like the Pope, the President, Lenin, Morgan or the King
become ideas and institutions." Furthermore, it is the abundant
and bewildering variety of our impressions, even after they have
been sifted or censored in all kinds of ways that tend to force
us to adopt the greater economy of the allegory, the picture or
story that can be interpreted to reveal hidden meanings. Since
we cannot, or it is difficult to, keep so many things vividly in
mind, we tend to group and name them and let the name stand
for the whole impression.[21]

But the mental processes do not stop there. A name is porous. "Old meanings slip out and new ones slip in, and the attempt to retain the full meaning of the name is almost as fatiguing as trying to recall the original impressions."[22] A name is also "a poor currency for thought.... And, so we begin to see the name through some personal stereotype, and to read into it, finally to see in it the incarnation or some human quality."[23]

Lippmann goes on to say that since "human qualities are themselves vague and fluctuating, they are best remembered by a physical sign." Therefore, "the human qualities we tend to ascribe to the names of our impressions themselves tend to be visualized in physical metaphors." Lippmann illustrates:

> The people of England, the history of England, condense into England, and England become John Bull, who is jovial and fat, not too clever, but well able to take care of himself. The migration of a people may appear to some as the meandering of a river, and to others like a devastating flood. The courage people display may be objectified as a rock; their purpose as a road, their doubts as forks of the road, their difficulties as ruts and rocks, their progress as a fertile valley. If they mobilize their dreadnaughts, they un-sheath a sword. If their army surrenders, they are thrown to earth. If they are oppressed, they are on the rack or under the harrow.[24]

The political columnist/commentator, advocate journalist, functioning as visualizer, creates such metaphors—words or phrases applied to an object, event, or action—in the persuasion process.

The third required skill is to be able to understand the target audience. Lippmann also provides the practitioner of *Real Advocacy Journalism*™ with clues as to what traits or characteristics he/she can expect a contemporary audience to have.

Lippmann raises—through a series of advocatory questions—critical issues to be considered in adapting discourse in audiences to accomplish specific purposes. Asks Lippmann: "How then is any practical relationship established between what is in the people's heads and what is out there beyond their ken in the environment? How in the language of democratic theory do great numbers of people feeling each so privately about so abstract a picture, develop any common will? How does a simple and constant idea emerge from this complex of variables? How are those things known as the Will of the People, or the National Purpose, or Public Opinion crystalized out of such fleeting and casual imagery?"[25]

It is necessary for the political columnist/commentator, the practitioner of *Real Advocacy Journalism*™, to begin any attempt at shaping public opinion by recognizing the triangular relationship between "the scene of action, the human picture of that scene, and the human response to that picture working itself out upon the scene of action."[26] Lippmann says "it is like a play suggested to the actors by their own experience, in which the plot is transacted in the real lives of the actors, and not merely in their stage parts. The moving picture often emphasizes with great skill this double drama of interior motive and external behavior."[27] For example: "Two men are quarrelling, ostensibly about some money, but their passion is inexplicable. Then the picture fades out and what one or the other of the two men sees with his mind's eye is re-enacted. Across the table they were quarrelling about money. In memory, they are back in their youth when the girl jilted him for the older man. The exterior drama is explained: The hero is not greedy; the hero is in love."[28]

It must be recognized by the advocate journalist, therefore, that the identical story, the same event, is not necessarily the same story or the same event to all who hear or witness it. Each person will enter the story or event at a slightly different point, since no two experiences are exactly alike. Each person will also re-enact the story or event in his/her own way and transfuse it with his/her own feelings. Lippmann reminds us that, "rarely does an artist of compelling skill force us to enter into lives altogether unlike our own lives that seem at first glance dull, repulsive, or eccentric."

In almost every story that catches our attention, "we become a character and act out the role with a pantomime of our own. The pantomime may be subtle or gross, may be sympathetic to the story, or only crudely analogous; but it will consist of those feelings which are aroused by our conception of the role. And so, the original theme as it circulates, is stressed, twisted, and embroidered by all the minds through which it goes. It is as if a play of Shakespeare's were rewritten each time it is performed with all the changes of emphasis and meaning that the actors and audience inspired."[29]

With these tendencies of variations of perceptions, we can conclude that the more mixed the audience, the greater will be the variation in the response. "For as the audience grows larger, the number of common words diminishes. Thus, the common factors in the story become more abstract." The story, therefore, "lacking precise character of its own, is heard by people of highly varied character. They give it their own character."[30] Furthermore, the character that the member of the audience gives it varies not only with sex and age, race and religion and social position, but within these cruder classifications, it varies according to "the inherited and acquired constitution of the individual, his faculties, his career, the progress of his career, an emphasized aspect of his career, his moods and tenses, or his place on the board in any of the games of life that he is playing. What reaches him of public affairs, a few lines of print, some photographs, anecdotes, and some casual experience of his own, he conceives through his set patterns and recreates with his own emotions."[31]

Lippmann is saying to the political columnist/commentator, the shaper of public opinion, the practitioner of *Real Advocacy Journalism*™, that he/she must have some understanding of the people he/she is attempting to influence; he/she must be aware of what they think they know, what their experiences are and the nature of their perceptions. The practitioner of *Real Advocacy Journalism*™ whose purpose is to persuade must make some attempt to appraise not only the information which has been at his/her audience's disposal, but the minds through which that information has been filtered. For the accepted stereotypes, the current social patterns, the standard versions, intercept information on its way to consciousness.

Did Lippmann as a practitioner of *Real Advocacy Journalism*™ disentangle ideas? Did he function as visualizer? Did he adjust his discourse to the needs of his audience?

The advocate journalist must be good at disentangling ideas, of naming, of creating symbols, and establishing common ground. This is true whether the target audience is large or small. The need to form some kind of common identity, a bridge that all can relate and feel comfortable walking across, is paramount. Upon disentangling the ideas, and effectively naming, the advocate journalist must be very capable of being a visualizer, presenting pictures and images that bring about strong emotions and personal identification. Knowing the target audience will inform the advocate journalist as he/she explains ideas and create visual images.

These three abilities—naming and disentangling words and ideas, effective visualizing and creating pictures of those words and ideas and understanding the target audience—are critical requirements in the arsenal of an effective political columnist/commentator, the advocate journalist, the consummate practitioner of *Real Advocacy Journalism*™.

7

REAL ADVOCACY JOURNALISM™
IN THE TWENTY-FIRST CENTURY:
RULES OF ENGAGEMENT

Walter Lippmann was an architect in twentieth-century journalism. He single-handedly established a type of discourse which has become a dominant part of the public communication process. Lippmann labored to show on a theoretical and philosophical level how a genre of discourse best described as *Real Advocacy Journalism*™—not just advocacy journalism as it was initially called—is needed in contemporary society in the presentation and resolution of public issues and the establishment of public policies. He endeavored for almost a half-century to apply his theoretical and philosophical postulates to the situations around him, to test them, to see if they would work in making government, society, function better.

As a philosopher, as a theoretician, Lippmann demonstrated how the complexity of society, the inadequacy of information flow, and man's propensity to function in pseudo-environments preclude him from making intelligent decisions on complicated public issues. Because of these exigencies there is a pressing need for someone to order, to interpret, to synthesize, to judge those events, those issues impacting contemporary man's surroundings.

Contemporary man, more so than at any point in history, needs to be prepared, educated, and guided to think along the proper lines. Often, he needs to be told not only how to think, but what to think in order to respond intelligently when called upon to participate in deciding public policies. When a complicated issue arises, he must be advised. He must be told what the good is, and what actions to take in reference to acquiring that good.

It is through *Real Advocacy Journalism*™—that genre of discourse which attempts to pull everything together, put events into their proper and accurate perspective in order to bring about the right and good end, and the expedient and proper course of action—that the potential for error in judgment on public matters is minimized.

The political columnist/commentator, as a practitioner of *Real Advocacy Journalism*™, strives to help clarify, to evaluate, and draw conclusions for his/her readers/listeners who have been too preoccupied, too removed from actual events to judge clearly for themselves. The political columnist/commentator shares the results of his/her either having witnessed things first-hand, or his/her having been privy to first-hand information, experts, and key people directly involved in the issue under discussion. Through the eyes and experiences of the political columnist/commentator, the reader/listener is able to become knowledgeable, to experience, to visualize, to understand, to arrive at an opinion about what is going on in his/her community, in his/her country, in the world.

In this respect, the political columnist/commentator has a direct influence on the formation of public opinion. In the case of Walter Lippmann, we have seen that his purpose was to influence public opinion, and, ultimately, the course of public policy. In fact, he felt this was the obligation and responsibility of those, who like himself, had special gifts or insights. It is clear, Lippmann likened his purpose to that of a mission. He felt that the citizenry generally had neither the time, the ability, nor the inclination to inform itself on important questions affecting the country or the world. Contemporary society was simply too great, and man's immediate environment too dominant, too consuming. Someone had to sort it all, lend direction, give advice.

Lippmann wrote his political column on the assumption that those who read him turned to him for logic and enlightenment. He felt a moral duty to deal with an issue in reference to practical consequences and alternatives. He once said, "It is not enough to criticize the official's policy. We must adjust ourselves inside his skin for unless we have tried to face up to the facts before him, what we produce is nothing but holier-than-thou moralizing."[1]

Speaking at the National Press Club on his seventieth birthday, Lippmann made his position quite clear: "If the country is to be governed with the consent of the governed, then the governed must arrive at opinions about what their governors want them to consent to." How do they do this? During the time of Lippmann, the public primarily arrived at opinions from listening to the radio, reading the newspapers, and later watching television, to access what the corps of correspondents told them was going on in Washington, in the country at large, and in the world. Lippmann emphasized that "here we perform an essential service . . . we do what every sovereign citizen is supposed to do but has not the time or the interest to do for himself. This is our job. It is no mean calling, and we have a right to be proud of it and to be glad that it is our work."[2] This is true of journalists as well as political columnists/commentators.

While today, the public is bombarded with opinions espoused on TV, radio, and the Internet—including social media and blogs—the responsibility of those proffering and promoting positions is no less weighty. But, too often, what is heard or read are biased, unbalanced, if not downright false, arguments presented by those who are more interested in a specific outcome of an issue, an organizational or partisan political agenda, even sheer propaganda. Unfortunately, this type of discourse is being passed off as *Real Advocacy Journalism*™, when it violates the standards and practices of what *Real Advocacy Journalism*™, as Lippmann codified it, is all about. *Real Advocacy Journalism*™, when practiced as it should be is about presenting objective facts, the path to truth, understanding and knowledge upon which the public can arrive at the best decision and course of action.

When the author asked James Reston in an interview what constituted public knowledge for Lippmann and how does the public come to know enough to make responsible decisions? Reston responded: "He [Lippmann] says in effect that we are the eyes and the ears of people. And that even though there are thoughtful and concerned people in Chicago or Madison, Wisconsin, or wherever, they can't be here [in Washington]. They can't be in on my lunch with [Zbigniew] Brzezinski [Former National Security Council Assistant to President Carter for National Security affairs], so, in effect, I am their surrogate. I gather some information and have opportunities to gather information they don't and share it with them. And that is the 'compacted' truth. And that is what he [Lippmann] thought. People can't be everywhere, have access to the Polish Ambassador or head of the Polish desk here, or go and talk to the Czech Ambassador of what he thinks about this uproar on his borders. This is really what we do."[3]

Lippmann was always seeking that median, that moral, ethical, and practical balance where man with his fellow man could work to promote the good society. As one author describes it: "Lippmann's most important fight has been his long battle against the darkness in men's minds. He has pleaded for sanity in a period of hysteria, moderation in the place of intemperance, and the rigors of thought instead of easy surrenders to partisanship."[4]

James Reston sees Lippmann's writings as having an added dimension more so than the typical political columnist. Reston feels that Lippmann perceived his own role as having a some- what loftier purpose than the average columnist. According to Reston, Lippmann "has a somewhat different view of his role." There was a close correlation between what Lippmann wrote in his books and what he wrote in his daily columns, and Reston describes this correlation:

> [Lippmann] used the news of the day in order to develop his philosophic series. He had strong and deep views run- ning back in his studies for many, many years.... Really since his days in Harvard.... About the nature of society: How it should be organized. You see by the titles of his books, *The Good Society*..., even studying this ever since he had been in Harvard with Santayana and William James. And what he did was primarily to use whatever happened in the news at that particular time in order to develop his own analysis of it, but usually in relation to his philosophy. In that sense, he was a much deeper columnist than anybody else of his time or our present time. There hasn't been anyone to compare with him. So, I would say, yes [he was] an educator; he thought of it as an educational procedure. That's what he did when he was on the *New Republic*, that's what he did as an editorial writer at the *World* and then he went over to do "Today and Tomorrow."[5]

To illustrate, Reston spoke of how Lippmann would analyze the situation in Poland if he were writing in the early 1980s when Poland was in crisis: "He wouldn't be analyzing whether the Red Army was going to go into Poland or not go into Poland. He might write about the tragedy of Poland, about how its bow has been caught between the giants, between the Germans, the Nazis and now the Communists on the other side. Or he might write about the enduring power of the faith in the Catholic Church among the Polish people. Or he might write about the failure of the authoritarian state. The fact that they got into this mess in Europe, merely proves that two generations after the war, the Communist society is simply not working. But this would be the longer-range way of looking at it."[6]

Lippmann functioned as a man who took time to ponder the universal and particular questions of contemporary society by painstakingly developing a philosophy, the basis of which was used to measure and analyze specific issues. This gave his columns something more than a momentary or fleeting meaning.

While Lippmann had no peer, he had many emulators and thus had a major impact on the development of *Real Advocacy Journalism*™ as a much-needed genre of public discourse. What was the nature of the columnists who came on the scene after Lippmann's impact over nearly four decades, from early 1932 to late 1967?

Contemporary political columnists were generally considered as successors to the great tradition of "personal journalism." They were identified or at least remotely associated with such "personal journalists" as Isaiah Thomas, Thomas Paine, John Fenno, Phillip Feneav, Horace Greeley, James Gordon Bennett, Henry J. Payomond, Charles A. Dana, and Joseph Pulitzer. Some of Lippmann's contemporaries were Walter Winchell, Westbrook Pegler, and Drew Pearson.[7]

As their famous predecessors, contemporary columnists—who came on the scene during and since Lippmann's reign and several decades hence—have given a *distinctly individual interpretation* (emphasis added) of what is happening in the news, and other social, political, and economic events occurring in the world. Most enjoy personal followings of varying sizes.

Assessing columnists during the fifties, David Weingast observed that generally to their readers, the columnists "are experts on public affairs, possessing extraordinary powers of insight, if not of divination. They are widely quoted to support or contest prevailing views. They help, in short, to fashion public opinion."[8]

Characterizing the columnist back in 1944, Charlie Fisher said he/she is the "autocrat of the most prodigious breakfast table ever known." The columnist is "the voice beside the cracker barrel amplified to transcontinental dimensions. He is the only non-political figure of record who can clear his throat each day and say, 'Now, here's what I think...' with the assurance that millions will listen."[9] Fisher describes the successful columnist as one who "engages the instant daily attention of a greater number of clients than any author who ever set quill pen to paper or explored the keyboard of an Underwood with burning forefingers. The broadcasting of his notions is without parallel in the history of print."[10]

According to Fisher, columnists were able to gain this stature because they capitalized on the complexity, confusion, or turmoil of the times:

> The economic depression of the thirties seemed to give the men who were adroit in the handling of ideas their fast semblance of indispensability. In a time of torment and confusion, with the smell of war ever on the air from abroad, readers by the millions sought for someone who could answer all questions and explain all tangles. The columnists volunteered, each according to his gifts. If an employer or workman looked nervously toward Washington, in uneasiness or hope, he could find a daily dispatch interpreting the activity of the moment and making the future as clear and simple as a crystal ball. Another writer would reduce a labor problem

involving three million men to seven hundred lucid words. Searching among others, the reader could find one to fan his anger or sustain his belief or support his misgivings.[11]

Richard Weiner, writing in 1977 of syndicated columnists, asserts that "the personal recommendations of a columnist often are more influential than the more formal, impersonal opinions expressed on the editorial page. Readers feel a kinship with their favorite columnists, whether they are pundits or serious essayists, which they rarely feel with the editors and publishers who appear to operate from a loftier position."[12]

Back then, Weiner took his analysis of contemporary political columnists and assessed the impact of the advent of television on their role. According to Weiner, television [had] not hurt newspapers as much as one might think and certainly not in the sphere of columnists." And "despite the assertions of the broadcast media and its proponents, newspapers still are the dominant news source."[13] Television's primary attraction in terms of reporting news was, and continues to be, its ability to attract and "gather" enormous numbers of people to watch simultaneously the coverage of special events, such as space voyages, elections, and championship games of popular sports. It is the "action medium, a powerful dramatic means of involving audiences of all ages." But the drawback of early television was that on a day-in-day-out basis, more adults read local newspapers than watch television news broadcasts. Of course, today, that is no longer the case with the advent of twenty-four-hour cable news and continuous access to the Internet via computers, notepads/tablets, and smart phones.

Weiner also argued that even the longer one-hour TV news programs or documentaries present only brief, sketchy versions of the news as compared to the quantity and variety in most daily newspapers. So, the devoted news watcher or news buff often watch network and local newscasts and they avidly read about the same events in newspapers, for fuller details and sometimes for corroboration, as well as interpretation. And to some older adults, who grew up during the pre-television era, an event is fascinating when seen on television, but somehow isn't confirmed "until the newsprint is 'felt.'" Many newspapers were regarded with a level of respect not accorded televlsion.[14] Today, that situation is almost totally reversed with the continual decline of the newspaper print industry and the continued meteoric reliance on cable news and the Internet.

Walter Lippmann, himself, felt that the advent of television had not minimized or replaced the role of the columnist but rather enhanced the need for him/her. In an interview, Lippmann said: "Television is guilty of an awful lot of things in our lives, and one is its adding to the irrationality of the world, I think. There is no doubt of that because it makes everything simpler or more dramatic or more immediate than it is. You really, if you listen to television, can't find out what's going on in the world." The interviewer responded: "So with that you would merely imply that columnists and analysts are more important today than they ever were." Lippmann replied: "Yes, they are. They've got to stand against a tremendous tide, and I think they probably will." The interviewer then asked: "Do you think newspapers are here to stay? Lippmann responded: "Oh, yes. People can't live on television. I listen to the news on the television and it's very good. People like Walter Cronkite and David Brinkley are excellent, really, but you can't live on what they give you."[15]

What would Lippmann say today about the decline of print news and the meteoric rise of cable news, the Internet, and social media as major sources of public information? He would likely be pleased at print media's increasing online presence, providing similar detailed coverage with the capacity to reach a broader local, regional, national, and worldwide audience simultaneously. This all requires that the columnist be even more circumspect and diligent in assessing issues and conditions and delivering responsible comment and guidance to a public that is even more bombarded with accurate and inaccurate information. This is further compounded by complex forces impacting their personal lives and environments, and a global stage filled with actors and events that punctuate their lives on a daily basis, at any given time.

Whether functioning in the realm of print media, radio, television, or online, what can and should the serious shapers/ influencers of public opinion incorporate in such a needed and noble vocation and practice, if in fact, the goal is to bring about good ends and good outcomes, which could lead to a better society?

The genre of *Real Advocacy Journalism*™ is analytical and prescriptive in its approach in that its purpose is to put all aspects of an event, situation, or issue into perspective in order to foster understanding and provide direction for opinion or action. This is exemplified in Lippmann's works. *Real Advocacy Journalism*™ has been distinguished from the traditional genres of advocatory discourse—deliberative, judicial, and epideictic— in that the political columnist in formulating his/her discourse uniquely combines elements of all three traditional genres in order to present his/her audience with the most complete, most comprehensive, and balanced picture on the subject matter under discussion.

This means that the political columnist in the development of a position on any given issue, must perform a judicial act by urging that some assessment be made, on the part of the reader/ listener, about relevant past and present events surrounding an issue in terms of their accurateness, justness, or goodness.

This is generally done, particularly in the case of Lippmann, by offering historical and current examples and analogies. Concomitantly, a judgment must be rendered, not only on that historical event, but also on the present state of affairs, or present act, deed, or condition—whatever factors kindled the need for discussion and decision to take place, whatever advocatory situation warranted the intervention of the political columnist. And of course, the enlightenment is offered by the political columnist in the deliberation process where the advantages and disadvantages of a course of action are weighed for the immediate as well as long-range future, using contemporaneous incidents, conditions, relatable language, and symbols.

From an examination of Lippmann's works we have found that the genre of *Real Advocacy Journalism*™ is directed at two kinds of audiences: decision-makers, as well as spectators, instead of one or the other. Such discourse is directed to the decision-makers because they are the direct actors. They create. They determine. It is also directed to the spectators because they are the supportive bystanders. They are in a position to lend support, to align themselves with one side or the other.

There is a less tangible characteristic of *Real Advocacy Journalism*™, and it is also found in Lippmann's discourse. *Real Advocacy Journalism*™ connotes authoritativeness, and the political columnist seems to assume the role of an authority, an expert, one of light and leading. The presumption is made that he/she is read for logic, enlightenment, direction, and he/she has a mission to fulfill that expectation. The political columnist, for some reasons, whether the reasons can be articulated or not, is, or should be, capable and qualified to assess, to advise, to prescribe. The political columnist has been endowed, by experience, devoted study, a divine overseer, or any combination thereof to be about the business of enlightening and leading the masses. And the political columnist, therefore, warrants an attentive ear.

How many of today's political columnists, television commentators, radio talk show hosts, online bloggers fit this description? How many are accurately practicing *Real Advocacy Journalism*™?

A sense of mission is also implied by the nature of *Real Advocacy Journalism*™. The political columnist is or should be about the mission of leading mankind toward ends and good actions, which will ultimately help man, government, and society work better. The political columnist, through his/her discourse, is to or should prevent a disastrous or catastrophic turn of events from occurring, or certainly warn, admonish, or simply bring about awareness in his/her readers.

Whether the intent of the genre of *Real Advocacy Journalism*™ is being met by the many practitioners today across all the communication media outlets that are available to the public needs more investigation. It is a question that warrants consideration by all caring consumers of the cacophony of opinions with which they are bombarded on a constant basis.

But for now, it is certain that Walter Lippmann, an influential political columnist for nearly four decades, established the model as we know it, first, in twentieth-century America and for today. He has given the advocatory scholar and practitioner unparalleled guideposts of the form, the nature, and the impact of *Real Advocacy Journalism*™ as a vital aspect of public communication where the goal should always be to foster a good and healthy society, which we are still striving to achieve.

Some would argue that it would be unrealistic to expect journalists and political columnists today to have the wide-ranging and far-reaching influence that Walter Lippmann had for decades. The social and political challenges America and the world faced during Lippmann's time—two world wars, a major economic depression, a sustained cold war with the then powerful Soviet Union, the Korean and Vietnam wars, and racial unrest reaching an unprecedented crescendo—could be said to be more ominous and defining than those we are dealing with today. So far, we have managed to avoid another world war. We have also managed to avoid a massive and catastrophic economic depression, a new cold war, and there continues to be intermittent progress in race relations albeit intermittent and cyclical. While we may disagree about the state of the world back then and now, we all can agree that conditions, challenges, and our approaches to them are relative. Nonetheless, our challenges today are enormous. We are grappling to gain control of a global pandemic that has resulted in unprecedented rates of infections, deaths, loss of businesses, and a struggling economy with catastrophic effects. Public trust in government, our form of democracy, political leaders, the press is at an all time low. Racial divisions and hatred are on the rise.

We can deliberate endlessly about how the public and political environment today differ from those of Lippmann's time. We can deliberate endlessly about the advantages and disadvantages that exist today versus then. But there are some fundamental "take-aways" for new, aspiring, and seasoned practitioners of the business of influencing publics. The individual practitioner of *Real Advocacy Journalism*™ must:

- Be clear about why he/she wants to become a journalist, a political columnist/commentator, a pundit, politician, and influencer of public.
- Be clear about his/her purpose. Ask yourself: Do I truly care about the issue I am addressing for reasons beyond my selfish interests? Am I more concerned about how it might impact the well-being of the community, city, country, continent, the globe?
- Truly value the principles, policies, and practices that promote a good society.

- Be willing to devote the time, the effort to understand and become prepared to practice consistently the skills and use the resources that will ensure that he/she is functioning with the highest integrity, objectivity, purpose.
- Put in the research and effort to understand the history of the subject as well as the current condition/state about which he/she is explaining, advising, and/or promoting a position or a course of action.

In a time when the lines seem blurred between objective journalism, and what many are calling fake news, and responsible comment, the correct practice of *Real Advocacy Journalism*™ is needed more than ever to guide the public out of this morass. It is *Real Advocacy Journalism*™, as it should be executed, that will restore credibility to public discourse.

What defines and makes the genre of *Real Advocacy Journalism*™ honorable when it is practiced as it should be? One can know and be sure of some overriding characteristics:

- There need not be any conflict in objectivity when facts, truth, and an accurate accounting of reality are rendered in the process of communicating and persuading publics.
- False premises, misleading positions, myths, and other destructive messaging must be called out and debunked.
- The purpose and goals are always to inform, motivate readers/listeners to improve their lives, and on a broader scale that of their communities, their country, and society in general.
- When practiced correctly, *Real Advocacy Journalism*™ avoids being unbalanced, biased, or a propagandist arm for the interest of the few, the extreme.
- *Real Advocacy Journalism*™ is never confused with propaganda.

- Disclosures, disclaimers of biases and/or conflicts—real or the very appearance of—on the part of the practitioner of *Real Advocacy Journalism*™ are revealed to the audience. The audience is always better served by self-awareness and transparency.
- If the masses are to be successful in bringing about meaningful change, the correct practice of *Real Advocacy Journalism*™ will be one of the most effective means to bring it about.

The ultimate question: Will twenty-first century practitioners honor and adhere to the rules of engagement *Real Advocacy Journalism*™ requires, the needs of which Lippmann has so clearly described in his books, and so consistently practiced as he functioned as a journalist, pundit, political columnist?

Also, as an important byproduct, Lippmann has provided anchors and guidelines for politicians whom the public relies upon for understanding and promoting the best public policy. They would do well to apply the principles and characteristics of *Real Advocacy Journalism*™ as they espouse and vigorously promote positions on needed policies and legislation.

Will journalists, political columnists/commentators, pundits, and politicians, today, rise to their noble calling?

8

IMPACT OF LIPPMANN ON
AN ADVOCATE JOURNALIST:
A PERSONAL ACCOUNT

Note: This chapter contains excerpts from the author's memoir, From Liberty to Magnolia: In Search of the American Dream, *(2018).*

The tradition from my childhood days of gathering around the television and watching the evening news continued long after I had left home. In our household, and for years to follow, it seemed that Walter Cronkite and Eric Sevareid were the only newsman and commentator in existence. Cronkite anchored the *CBS Evening News* for nineteen years, from 1962 to 1981. During the turbulent 1960s and 1970s, he came to be known and was often characterized as "the most trusted man in America." This characterization was confirmed by opinion polls taken throughout his career. He became known for his extensive coverage of the major events over several decades, most notably the Cuban Missile Crisis, the assassinations of President John F. Kennedy, Attorney General Robert F. Kennedy, civil rights leader Martin Luther King Jr., the moon landing, and the resignation of President Richard Nixon.

Eric Sevareid, an author and award-winning journalist and commentator, delivered his first commentary on the *CBS Evening News with Walter Cronkite* on November 22, 1963, following the assassination of President John F. Kennedy. It was in 1964 that he began delivering a two-minute segment on *The CBS Evening News* on the important issues of the day. During his fourteen-year run, from 1964 to 1978, his insightful and inspiring commentary earned him both Emmy and Peabody Awards, among others. Also, Sevareid authored several books and hosted several television series in which he interviewed and profiled famous world leaders; newsmakers in business, politics, and the arts; and other influencers. But in my mind, his insightful commentary was his greatest contribution.

Eric Sevareid lit the flame within me to become a political columnist. Walter Lippmann set it ablaze.

Walter Lippmann died in 1974, shortly after I completed the course work and before I began writing my dissertation to complete the PhD degree. Even though I had access to all his works, including the original handwritten versions of his columns at the Sterling Hall Library at Yale, I wanted something more. I wanted to talk with some of his contemporaries. I thought of my inspiration, Eric Sevareid.

I took a long-shot chance and wrote Eric Sevareid a letter and recounted the experience with my mother, watching him on the evening news, and announcing to her when I was fourteen that someday I was going to do what Sevareid did. In the letter, I asked him if he would be so kind as to give me a few minutes of his time for a telephone interview. To my knee-buckling surprise, Mr. Sevareid, who by then had been retired from *The CBS Evening News* for a couple of years, telephoned me and invited me to his home in Chevy Chase, Maryland, where we visited for several hours.

I remember receiving Mr. Sevareid's call as if it were yesterday. I was sitting at my desk in the mayor's office in Milwaukee, Wisconsin, where I had taken a position on the staff of Mayor Henry Maier. At that time, Mayor Maier was one of the longest-tenured mayors of a major US city. Only Chicago Mayor Richard Daley had held office longer. Florence, the front-desk receptionist who had held that position for as long as Mayor Maier had been in office, came to the door and said, "I have Eric Sevareid on the line." Mayor Maier, who had entered my office a few moments earlier to discuss a budget issue looked at Florence and said, "Sevareid? What the hell does Eric Sevareid want with me?" Florence said, "He's not calling for you, Mayor. He is calling for Janice."

A wave of panic came over me. I jumped up, began walking in circles patting my chest, and thinking to myself, *I am going to sound like a babbling idiot.*

I took the call. I will never forget that voice on the other end of the line—that calming voice I had listened to for so many years as a teenager and well into adulthood. I picked up the phone and in my typical salutation, said, "Hello. This is Janice Anderson." He began, "Janice, this is Eric Sevareid. How are you?" Before I could answer, thank God, he continued, "I received your wonderful letter. I would be happy to meet with you. Call my assistant and schedule some time. Are you able to come to Chevy Chase to my home? It is located just outside of Washington, DC." All I can recall saying is, "Certainly. Certainly. Thank you, sir." He gave me his assistant's name and telephone number and ended the call by saying, "I look forward to meeting and visiting with you." In a daze, I think I said, "Me, too." He followed with, "Enjoy the rest of your day."

To which I said, in a muted but amazed tone, "Thank you. You too, sir." The phone went silent. He had to have known he had more than made my day.

My distant and chance encounter with a nationally and internationally respected journalist and political columnist/commentator, my first mentor, was about to become up close and personal.

It was mid-October. Later that day, I spoke with Mr. Sevareid's assistant and we set the meeting for the afternoon of December 8 at 10:00 a.m. This was in 1980. After the interview with Mr. Sevareid had been set, I called the noted columnist James Reston, who wrote for the *New York Times,* and arranged an interview with him in his Washington, DC, office for 2:00 p.m. on the same day.

When I arrived at the Sevareid home, in my best business suit with briefcase and tape recorder in hand, I was greeted by his housekeeper who invited me to come in. I waited in the foyer of his stately but warm home. Mr. Sevareid, tall and thin in a cream-colored turtleneck sweater, bigger than life, immediately came down a winding staircase. Like an astonished child, I stood there, a twenty-seven-year-old woman, and dropped my tape recorder. He rushed to me, picked it up, and said as he was handing the recorder to me, "We had better pray that the bloody thing works."

As I stood awestruck, he extended his hand and said, "How are you? I am Eric Sevareid. Welcome to my home." I was still speechless. Thankfully, he filled in the silence and said, "You must be Janice Anderson." (Anderson was my married name at the time.) After extending my hand, I responded quietly, "Yes. Pleased to meet you, sir." To this day, I remember standing there with mouth slightly agape, staring at this person I had watched for years on the national evening news and who had become in no small measure my mentor, albeit in absentia. He invited me into the sitting room where he asked his housekeeper to bring us tea.

We sat on his couch and spoke about Walter Lippmann's career as well as his own. He made it clear that he, like Lippmann, had a twofold purpose in writing his columns, which was "to elucidate and to advocate to achieve the greatest good for the greatest number in whatever situation or circumstance." Sevareid said to me, "In my own case, I've always attempted a training of my audience. I always lean to the function of trying to elucidate and advocate a position."

Sevareid went on to observe that many columnists make the mistake of assuming that people have much more information and understanding than they actually do. During our conversation, he offered this analogy: "Ray Clapper used to be a political columnist here in Washington, a very good one, for many years. He always used to say that you should never underestimate the intelligence of your audience and never overestimate their information."

Little did Mr. Sevareid know that his goal of elucidating and advocating had left a lasting impression on me, beginning when I was a teenager back in that little Mississippi farmhouse. He had inspired the calling within me to do what he did, which has lasted to this day. Often over the years, I have thought about our sitting together on his couch that unbelievable, euphoric, and exhilarating day. I still wonder whether I adequately conveyed to him during our precious time together his profound influence on what I wanted to do with my life.

While I was so very fascinated with him, he seemed to be a little curious and fascinated with me, too, which came as a pleasant surprise. He was curious about my family, my childhood, my journey from Mississippi, and why I wanted to be a columnist. I shared with him some of the major influences of my life growing up and during my college years—racial segregation, the promulgation of the idea of white supremacy, gender inequality, the poverty and deprivation that engulfed blacks, education inequality—and how I felt compelled to try to do something about it. I told him how I had been writing commentary for one of the largest radio stations in Wisconsin and a local newspaper for several years.

He asked how I had managed to start writing and delivering commentary for the radio station. I recounted that experience in detail. I told him, I decided to walk into the largest radio station in the State of Wisconsin, WISN Radio, and an ABC affiliate. Hal Walker, the program producer and director of public affairs agreed to meet with me in his office. After greeting me, I thanked Mr. Walker and told him that the purpose of my meeting was to ask for airtime to deliver my own commentary. I told him that I was thinking about something like a two-minute spot. He frowned, paused, looked at me, braced, and not surprisingly, asked, "Who the hell are you?"

Appearing unflappable and undeterred, but underneath my impregnable façade as nervous as I could be, I began to tell him about my background, my training, my passion. I told him how I thought we all have gifts and talents, and that mine was analyzing complex and tough issues and explaining them in a way that people can understand and perhaps get a perspective for a way forward.

Then I said, "May I show you some samples of my writing?" Still appearing stunned at my boldness, he frowned even more and extended his hand. I gave him my sample columns. To my surprise, he began to read them right then and there. After he had finished reading two of them and was reading the third one, he leaned back in his chair, looked at me, and said, "Will you excuse me for a moment?" I said, "Certainly."

By this time, my heart was in my throat. I knew he had left our meeting to figure out how to tell this "ballsy, brazen, whatever" woman he most assuredly thought me to be that I would not be getting airtime on his station.

After about ten minutes he returned. He walked back into his office, sat down, and said, "Well, young lady, we are going to give you a try." He offered me time to deliver a two-minute commentary. He clearly saw that I was stunned and speechless. He asked, "When can you come in to do a sample recording? What are you going to call it?" I just looked at him, still speechless. He followed, "Think about it. You will have to call it something." He looked at me and I still looked at him but didn't answer. "Well, just think about it and let's meet again in about a week or so. At that time, we will know more details about how often the commentary will be aired, what time, and the schedule for recording the spots in advance of their airing. In the meantime, call the recording studio and do a demo tape delivering one of these so we can see how you sound." He stood up and extended his hand. I stood up, I thanked him profusely, and he walked me to the door. I got into my car, sat behind the wheel, and began to clap my hands, screaming for joy and shouting, "Thank you, God. Thank you, God."

Ultimately, I settled on calling the spot, "The Janice Anderson Outlook." I went back and met with the producer the following week. I learned that the spots had to be recorded a week before they were to be aired. At first, I thought that requirement would pose a serious challenge for delivering timely content. But it proved to be fortuitous. It meant I had to select and write about issues that were systemic and of long-standing significance, not some fleeting incident or topic that faded or lost relevance at the end of a day. It also meant I had to take the longer view in addressing any issue I chose to write about.

During the 1970s, there was no shortage of significant topics to write about, whether in the areas of politics and government, public education, race relations, or women's issues. How did I debut the long-awaited opportunity to do what Sevareid and Lippmann did? As I wrote and delivered my first commentary on January 20, 1975, not surprisingly, the influence of both Sevareid and Lippmann was at the forefront of my mind. I felt I had to begin with a subject area that both had spent their lives trying to address in some way, and one about which resonated with me back then, and which remains a major concern today. "Politics as a Spectator Sport" was the subject of the first commentary I delivered.

I wrote and delivered commentary for the radio station for the next two years until I took a position with the mayor's office. To my dismay, I had to give up the commentary because the mayor thought any commentary I delivered going forward could be misconstrued as speaking on his behalf.

Perhaps as Mr. Sevareid listened to me he wondered how this black woman from Mississippi and the daughter of a poor black farmer came to be sitting on his couch discussing his career and that of the famed Walter Lippmann—and had the unmitigated temerity to think she could try to do what he and Lippmann did. Could that thought have crossed his mind? Perhaps. But I remember beaming when Mr. Sevareid gazed at me with those steely eyes and said, "With your passion and preparation, you can really make a difference as a columnist." He went on to ask whether I had reached out to Elizabeth Midgley, Walter Lippmann's long-time personal assistant and Marquis Childs, another renowned contemporary columnist who wrote for the *St. Louis Post-Dispatch*. I told him I had not, and that I had only reached out to James Reston whom I would be meeting with that afternoon. He volunteered to make calls to both Childs and Midgley on my behalf. I followed up and secured interviews with both Ms. Midgley and Mr. Childs.

Upon leaving Mr. Sevareid's home, I was filled with exhilaration and the resolve to finish my dissertation about Lippmann as soon as possible; and to continue writing my own column in an attempt to have an impact on the issues confronting the public and make a difference with the ultimate goal of syndication.

As I worked feverishly to complete my dissertation, periodically, I would be seized by the question: What could I take away from the prolific and profound works of Walter Lippmann? I concluded, a lot. But my first challenge was to get my arms around it all, make sense of it, identify the relevance, compile the findings, and create a document that my five-member doctoral committee would find worthy enough to award the PhD degree.

There were times, while wading through the voluminous works of Lippmann and other research about him, that the thought of completing the PhD seemed like an impossibility, with raising two sons alone, writing a commentary for a local radio station and newspaper, and working a demanding job in a mayor's office. When I finally embarked on writing the dissertation, years had passed since I had completed the required course work for the degree. More often than not, during that time, I felt laden with thoughts about Lippmann as if I were carrying around a heavy weight in my head that I could never find the time to put down on paper. Or, like the elephant, I was pregnant with this massive creation that was taking years to take shape into a viable and meaningful entity. There were times I wondered if I ever *would* give birth to my dissertation, which weighed me down.

But after years of research, with life often getting in the way, and snatching blocks of time at every opportunity to organize my findings, I knew Lippmann had so much to offer—not only for me, in achieving my dream of becoming a good political columnist, but also for all who aspire to become effective political columnists. My looming task was to cull, carve out, and capture the relevant elements of his voluminous work.

When I wrote my first column for WISN Radio, after having just completed my course work for my PhD, I did not feel overwhelmed by the social, political, and educational issues playing out on the world stage about which I was going to write. I felt a sense of empowerment instead. I owed that feeling of preparedness, no doubt, to having been immersed in the writings of Walter Lippmann.

While the problems and issues may have been daunting, I felt that finding the solutions was not beyond our reach. I was convinced that the life and works of Walter Lippmann offered valuable lessons for a path forward.

Walter Lippmann's Lasting Influence on Me

As a practicing political columnist, concerned with influencing public opinion and the shape of public policy, Lippmann had overriding concepts and basic beliefs about what the role of the political analyst should be, and what basic functions he or she is to perform in the process of enlightening the public and effectuating persuasion on key issues. These concepts and beliefs were like a clarion call about what I should be doing, and how.

I had to be or become very good at separating words and their meaning, as well as disentangling ideas. I had to be or become and effective visualizer—be able to create accurate representations of ideas or matters that are ordinarily invisible to contemporary man or normally out of his reach. I kept thinking about what a noble calling I was about to embark upon.

I knew then how difficult it was going be to unmask and address issues like racism, sexism, educational disparities, economic disparities, and all the social conditions that were causing the chasms and great divides I saw around me. I remember thinking how difficult the disentanglement process was going to be and the monumental task of building a bridge across which we all would be comfortable walking.

No matter how difficult, the process of naming, clarifying, and pinpointing had to be done, and done well. Naming things and assigning specific meanings or associations to words and ideas, helps the reader/listener relate and make connections. In addition, and more importantly, the recipient of the analysis will be better able to receive and understand the information and position being put forward. They will be better able to see how the condition being addressed impacts their lives, their family, community, state, and nation.

I found comfort in the notion that if the political columnist, during the process of persuasion, engaged in clarification, enlightenment, and re-education of this kind, it helped to form the correct opinion, consistent with the real issues at hand. This is the only way to fight against and replace incorrect facts, misperceptions, propaganda, and demagoguery.

I felt comfort and an obligation to make use of experts and other sources of research to ensure that the description or recommended courses of action were the most accurate, the most grounded, the best that they could be for the targeted audience and anyone who might be engaged.

I knew that my work was not about promoting my ideas or agenda. Rather, my work had to be about determining the meaning of a situation and untangling the conditions and circumstances that brought them about, enabling members of the public to act responsibly and appropriately instead of acting emotionally or with misinformation.

Lippmann also emphasizes the importance of the political columnist to be an effective visualizer, to be able to capture and convey accurately and vividly those ideas, events, and matters that are often invisible to the public, or normally beyond the public's reach, or out of the public's realm of immediate consciousness. The political columnist is to whet the audience's appetites, stimulate the creative and artistic faculties of those in attendance—all in an effort to enkindle a more complete understanding and, therefore, a fuller experience in the communication act. In other words, the political columnist is to act as visualizer to bring about the greatest degree of identification. This is done by trying to involve and stimulate as much of the audience's total consciousness as possible.

Could I be an effective visualizer? Would I be able to capture and convey ideas, events, issues, and possible solutions in a way that would capture and hold the reader's and listener's attention long enough to be informed, inspired, or motivated to act? For a while, I was seized with doubt. I began to wonder whether my analyses or writings would be good enough. After all, who was I?

For Lippmann, it is not enough for the political columnist just to visualize. The columnist must also feel something to get the total meaning and convey that meaning to others. The pieces, the actions, the players—all have to fit and must be addressed to get the full picture, as difficult as it might be to express. While feeling and intuition might play a role, they must be associated with facts and reasons.

Was I gifted enough? Could I rely on my intuition as a starting point? Would I be able to determine the right course, using intuition, facts, and reason as I addressed an issue? Would I be able to discern the right or reasonable path in a way that anyone would pay attention and be motivated sufficiently enough to form the right opinion, to act? I began to feel acutely the weight and responsibility of the work I so desperately wanted to be about. I knew that trying to follow in the footsteps of Sevareid or Lippmann was not an easy calling.

When actions depend on a group of people being of one mind or agreeing on the same course of action, it must have a visual or relatable value. The audience must feel similarly, have common buy-in. In essence, the audience must feel and experience the issue in a personal and similar way for its members to become truly engaged, for them to really care. An issue becomes important when it impacts our values, our well-being, and that of those we care about.

But as I completed my study, I was certain that Walter Lippmann, an influential political columnist for nearly four decades, is the man who established the model for *Real Advocacy Journalism*™ as it should be practiced in twenty-first-century America. He has given current and future political columnists, the practitioners of *Real Advocacy Journalism*™, unparalleled guideposts as to the nature, form, and the impact of this vital aspect of public communication, where the goal should always be to foster a good and healthy society, a search that continues today.

It is in the spirit of Walter Lippmann's work, and that of Eric Sevareid's, that I set out to do my best as a political columnist, as a woman of "light and leading."

In surveying my writings over the decades, their focus can be organized in three categories: Ethics and Values; Justice and Equality; and Patriotism and Politics, and I have compiled those commentaries in a three-book *Real Advocacy Journalism*™ series.

ADVANCING the GOOD SOCIETY: Real Advocacy Journalism™ *in Action*
Book I: Ethics and Values

ADVANCING the GOOD SOCIETY: Real Advocacy Journalism™ *in Action*
Book II: Justice and Equality

ADVANCING the GOOD SOCIETY: Real Advocacy Journalism™ *in Action*
Book III: Patriotism and Politics

In each book, the commentaries have been grouped under major section headings. I have begun each section with one of my very first commentaries that were written and delivered in a two-minute spot on WISN Radio, the largest ABC affiliate, located in Milwaukee, Wisconsin, during 1974-76. They have been chosen for their enduring relevancy. The remaining commentaries in each section have been written across the decades, and are included without dates, but rather chosen instead because of the *timeliness*, or *timelessness* of their subject matter—then and now. This series will be published in late 2021/early 2022.

I continue to write at https://janicesellis.com. Please join me there. I would love to see your comments and have a lively exchange as we work together to build a great society.

ABOUT THE AUTHOR

Janice S. Ellis, M.A., M.A., Ph.D., a native daughter of Mississippi, grew up and came of age during the height of the Civil Rights Movement and the Women's Liberation Movement. Born and reared on a small cotton farm, she was influenced by two converging forces that would set the course of her life.

The first was the fear and terror felt by blacks because of their seeking to exercise the right to vote along with other rights and privileges afforded whites. She became determined to take a stand and not accept the limits of that farm life nor the strictures of oppressive racial segregation and gender inequality. She aspired to have and achieve a different kind of life—not only for herself, but for others.

The second was her love of books, the power of words, and her exposure to renowned columnists Eric Sevareid of The CBS Evening News with Walter Cronkite and Walter Lippmann, whose column appeared for more than three decades in over 250 major newspapers across the United States and another 50 newspapers abroad.

It was the study of Lippmann's books and commentary that inspired Dr. Ellis to complete a Master of Arts degree in Communication Arts, a second Master of Arts degree in Political Science, and a Doctor of Philosophy in Communication Arts, all from the University of Wisconsin. It was during her course of study that Dr. Ellis' unwavering belief—the belief that the wise use of words is what advances the good society—was solidified.

Dr. Ellis has been an executive throughout her career, first in government, then in a large pharmaceutical company, later as President and CEO of a marketing firm, and finally as President and CEO of a bi-state non-profit child advocacy agency. Along with those positions, she has been writing columns for more than four decades on race, politics, education, and other social issues for a major metropolitan daily newspaper, *Kansas City Star*; a major metropolitan business journal, *Milwaukee Business Journal*; and for community newspapers *The Milwaukee Courier*, *The Kansas City Globe*, and *The Kansas City Call*. She wrote radio commentary for two years for one of the largest ABC radio affiliates in Wisconsin and subsequently wrote and delivered a two-minute spot on the two largest Arbitron-rated radio stations in the Greater Kansas City area. She has also written for several national trade publications, focusing on healthcare and the pharmaceutical industry.

Dr. Ellis published an online magazine, USAonRace.com, for seven years dedicated to increasing understanding across race and ethnicity, in which she analyzed race and equality issues in America. The website continues to attract thousands of visitors per year. The site also has a vibrant Facebook page with fans numbering in the thousands. Dr. Ellis launched a companion site, RaceReport.com, which aggregates news about race relations, racism, and discrimination from across the United States and around the world on a daily basis.

Dr. Ellis also has her own website, JaniceSEllis, which houses a collection of her writings and where she writes a regular blog. Follow her on facebook.com/janicesellis1/ and twitter.com/janicesellis1.

Her first book, *From Liberty to Magnolia: In Search of the American Dream* (**2018**) has received several national and international awards since its initial release. The most recent is the Independent Press Award for Race Relations (May 2020). It was noted that the competition is judged by experts from different aspects of the book industry, including publishers, writers, editors, book cover designers and professional copywriters. Selected award winners and distinguished favorites are based on overall excellence. In 2020, the Independent Press Award had entries worldwide. Participating authors and publishers reside in countries such as Australia, Brazil, Cambodia, Canada, India, Ireland, Portugal, Sweden, and others. Books submitted included writers located in cities such as Austin to Memphis to Santa Cruz; from Copenhagen to Mumbai; from Albuquerque to Staten Island; from Boise to Honolulu, and others.

Other international and national awards the book has received include: the New York City Big Book Award for Women Issues (November 2019); the Grand Prize Journey Award for Nonfiction (April 2019) from Chanticleer International Book Reviews; the Gold Medal Award for Nonfiction Books from the Non Fiction Authors Association (May 2018), the highest award bestowed for nonfiction authors. **From Liberty to Magnolia** received a notable editorial review and honor from Kirkus Reviews, one of the oldest and most credible reviewers of books for libraries, schools, bookstores, publishers, agents, and other industry professionals. In bestowing the honor, Kirkus noted, "*From Liberty to Magnolia* was selected by our Indie Editors to be featured in *Kirkus Reviews* April 15, 2018 Issue. Congratulations! Your review has appeared as one of the 35 reviews in the Indie section of the magazine which is sent out to over 5,000 industry professionals (librarians, publishers, agents, etc.) Less than 10% of our Indie reviews are chosen for this, so it's a great honor." The book continues to receive great customer reviews on Amazon and Goodreads.

Dr. Ellis' most recent book is *Shaping Public Opinion: How Real Advocacy Journalism*™ *Should Be Practiced.* (2021)

NOTES

Chapter One: Who Was Walter Lippmann?

1. Ronald Steel, *Walter Lippmann and the American Century* (Boston: Little, Brown and Co., 1980), p. XIV.
2. Walter Lippmann, *A Preface to Morals* (New York: The Macmillan Company, 1929), p. 318.
3. Ibid., pp. 319-320.
4. Walter Lippmann, "A Tribute to C. P. Scott," editor of the *Manchester Guardian*, published as a preface to "Newspaper Ideals," a pamphlet by Scott (New York: Halcyon Commonwealth Foundation, 1964). This can be found in the Walter Lippmann Papers at Yale University.
5. The following books are generally considered as Lippmann's most important works. A complete listing of his books is found in the bibliography: 1. *A Preface to Politics* (New York and London: Mitchell, Kennerly, 1913); 2. *A Preface to Morals* (New York: The Macmillan Company, 1929); 3. *Public Opinion* (New York: The Macmillan Company, 1922); 4. *Phantom Public* (New York: Harcourt, Brace and Company, 1925); 5. *The Good Society* (Boston: Little, Brown and Co., 1937); 6. *Essays in the Public Philosophy* (Boston: Little, Brown and Co., 1955).

6. Lippmann has published many articles during his career. A complete collection of the original and published copies of Lippmann's articles is found in the Walter Lippmann Papers, and the Robert O. Anthony Collection of Walter Lippmann, housed in the Manuscripts and Archives room at Sterling Memorial Library, Yale University. Magazines in which his articles appeared include: *The American Magazine, The American Scholar, The Annals of the American Academy of Political and Social Science, The Atlantic Monthly, The Commonwealth, Forum and Century, Earner's Magazine, The Harvard Monthly, Life, Look, Metropolitan, The New Republic, The Saturday Evening Post, Social Forces, Vanity Fair, Vital Speeches of the Day, Women's Home Companion, The Yale Review,* and *Newsweek.*

7. Lippmann's commentaries appeared in the *New York Herald Tribune* from 1930-1962 and in *The Washington Post* from 1963-1967. They were syndicated in one hundred and forty newspapers.

8. Clinton Rossiter and James Lare, *The Essential Lippmann* (New York: Random House, 1963), p. xx.

9. Rossiter and Lare, p. xx.

10. One can find this opinion expressed throughout *Walter Lippmann and His Times,* a compilation of essays written by Lippmann's contemporaries and edited by Marquis Childs and James Reston. (New York: Harcourt, Brace and Co., 1959). That opinion is also expressed in *The Essential Lippmann,* a collection of Lippmann's works edited by Clinton Rossiter and James Lare. (New York: Random House, 1963).

11. Rossiter and Lare, p. xiii.

12. James Reston in *Walter Lippmann and His Times,* p. 234.

13. Ibid.

14. Brown, John Mason, *Through These Men* (New York: Harper and Brothers, 1956). pp. 202-204.
15. Lippmann wrote many books between 1913 and 1965. Many of them represent key aspects of his thoughts at various stages of development. The books listed contain his most developed philosophical thought.
16. There are approximately 4,200 columns stored in forty-nine binders (eleven archival boxes) in the Robert O. Anthony Collection. The original copies are stored in fourteen boxes with the Walter Lippmann Papers.
17. David E. Weingast, *Walter Lippmann. A Study in Personal Journalism* (New Jersey: Rutgers University Press, 1949), p. 22.

Chapter Two: Lippmann the Political Columnist: A Real Advocate Journalist Emerges

1. Robert O. Anthony, *Index to the Robert 0. Anthony Collection of Walter Lippmann*, Vol. I, p. 13.
2. James Thurslow Adams, "Walter Lippmann," *The Saturday Review of Literature*, January 7, 1933. Vol. IX, No. 25, p. 361. Article found in the Walter Lippmann Collection, Box 19, Folder 409.
3. Robert O. Anthony, *Index to the Walter Lippmann Papers*, Vol. II, p. 135.
4. Robert O. Anthony, *Index to the Robert O. Anthony Collection of Walter Lippmann*, Vol. I, p. 94.
5. Henry Allen, "Chronicling Walter Lippmann," *The Washington Post*, September 11, 1980, p. Dl.
6. Marquis Childs, "Tribute to Walter Lippmann," *Quill*, October 1973, p. 16. Article found in the Robert O. Anthony Collection of Walter Lippmann, Box 18, Folder 404.

7. Steel made this statement in an interview with Henry Allen published in *The Washington Post*, September 11, 1980, "Chronicling Walter Lippmann," p. D13.
8. Thomas Griffith, "Comrade of the Powerful," Newswatch in *Time*, September 15, 1980, p. 86.

Chapter Three: Lippmann Evaluated as a Real Advocate Journalist

1. Robert O. Anthony, *Index to the Robert O. Anthony Collection of Walter Lippmann*, Vol. I, p. 12.
2. Doris Grumbach, "Five Print," *The New Republic*, January 25, 1975, p. 33.
3. Ronald Steel, *The New Republic*, December 28, 1974.
4. Joseph Kraft, "Lippmann, Yesterday, Today and Tomorrow," *The Washington Post*, September 11, 1980, p. A19.
5. Elizabeth Peer, "Walter Lippmann, 1889-1974," *Newsweek*, December 23, 1974. Article found in the Walter Lippmann Collection, Box 18, Folder 394, pp. 1 and 40.
6. *Time*, December 23, 1974. Walter Lippmann Collection, Box 18, Folder 395.
7. Harrison E. Salisbury, "Final Tribute," New *Times*, December 1974, p. 68. Walter Lippmann Collection, Box 18, Folder 396.
8. Elizabeth Peer, pp. 40-45.
9. *Times*, pp. 56-57.
10. Peter Prescott in *Newsweek*, September 8, 1980, p. 76.
11. Steel in an interview with Henry Allen, in *The Washington Post*, p. D13.
12. James Reston, "The Mockingbird and The Taxicab," in *Walter Lippmann and His Times*, edited by Marquis

Childs and James Reston, (New York: Harcourt, Brace and Co., 1959), p. 235.

13. Reston, in *Walter Lippmann and his Times*, p. 227.
14. Ibid.
15. Ibid.
16. Reston made this observation during an interview with Walter Lippmann, found in *Walter Lippmann and His Times*, p. 227.
17. Brown p. 217.
18. Ibid.
19. Lippmann quoted in Brown, p. 217.
20. Brown, pp. 226-227.
21. John Mason Brown, p. 199.
22. Brown, pp. 199-200.

Chapter Four: The Need, Role, and Function of *Real Advocacy Journalism*™

1. Walter Lippmann, *Essays in the Public Philosophy*, (Boston: Little, Brown and Co., 1955). Quoted from the reprinted version published by The American Library, Inc. p 96.
2. Ibid.
3. Ibid., p. 97.
4. Ibid.
5. Ibid.
6. Ibid., p. 98.
7. Ibid.
8. Walter Lippmann, *Public Opinion* (New York: Macmillan Co., 1922), p. 158.
9. Ibid.
10. Ibid.
11. Ibid.

12. Ibid.
13. Ibid.
14. Walter Lippmann, *An Inquiry Into Principles of the Good Society* (Boston: Little, Brown and Co., 1937) p. 26.
15. Ibid.
16. *Essays in the Public Philosophy*, p. 103.
17. Ibid.
18. Ibid., p. 99.
19. Walter Lippmann, *Liberty and the News* (New York: Harcourt, Brace and Howe, 1920), p. 63.
20. *Public Opinion*, p. 18.
21. Ibid., p. 53.
22. Ibid.
23. Ibid., p. 59.
24. Ibid., pp. 59-60.
25. Ibid.
26. Ibid., p. 59.
27. Ibid.
28. Ibid.
29. Ibid., p. 60.
30. Ibid.
31. Ibid.
32. Ibid., pp. 18-19.
33. Ibid., pp. 16-17.
34. Ibid., p. 16.
35. Ibid., p. 17.
36. Ibid., p. 111.
37. Ibid., p. 112.
38. Ibid., pp. 114-115.
39. Ibid., p. 111.
40. Ibid., pp. 111-112.
41. Reston-Anderson Interview, December 8, 1980.
42. Ibid.

43. Walter Lippmann, *Liberty and the News*, pp. 37- 38.
44. *Public Opinion*, p. 202.
45. Ibid., p. 203.
46. Ibid., p. 216.
47. Ibid., p. 218.
48. Ibid.
49. Ibid.
50. Ibid., p. 223.
51. Ibid.
52. Ibid., p. 226.
53. *Essays in the Public Philosophy*, p. 99.
54. Ibid.
55. Ibid.
56. Ibid.
57. *Public Opinion*, p. 229.
58. Ibid.
59. Ibid., pp. 229-230.
60. Ibid., p. 230.
61. Ibid.
62. Ibid.
63. Ibid., pp. 233-234.
64. Ibid., p. 236.
65. Ibid., p. 237.
66. Ibid., p. 238.
67. Ibid., p. 142.
68. Ibid., pp. 142-143.
69. Ibid., p. 143.
70. *Liberty and the News*, p. 85.
71. Ibid.
72. Ibid.
73. *Public Opinion*, p. 8.
74. Ibid., p. 142.
75. Ibid., p. 59.

76. Ibid., p. 254.
77. Ibid.
78. Ibid., p. 153.
79. Ibid.
80. Ibid.
81. Ibid., p. 150.
82. Ibid.
83. Ibid., p. 151.
84. Ibid.
85. Ibid., pp. 132-133.
86. Ibid., p.133.
87. Ibid.
88. Author's interview with Eric Sevareid.
89. Author's interview with James Reston.
90. Author's interview with Marquis Childs.
91. Lippmann, *The Cold War: A Study In U.S. Foreign Policy* (New York: Harper, 1947).
92. Brown pp. 200-201.
93. Reston, In *Walter Lippmann and His Times*, p. 237.
94. Holmes-Laski Letters quoted in Brown, p. 221.
95. Ibid.
96. Ibid.
97. The author interviewed Elizabeth Midgley, personal assistant to Walter Lippmann from January 1961-1967, in Washington, DC, January 27, 1981.
98. Author's interview with Reston.
99. The author interviewed Marquis Childs, Washington Columnist for the St. Louis Post-Dispatch in his office in Washington, DC, November 1, 1980.
100. The author interviewed Eric Sevareid, former CBS News Commentator in his home in the Washington Suburb of Chevy Chase, Maryland, on December 8, 1980.
101. Ibid., Brown, pp.202-203.

102. William Allen White, "Walter Lippmann Looks at the Political Scene," *New York Herald Tribune*, Oct. 23, 1932.
103. Weingast, pp. 30-31.
104. Midgley, an interview with author.
105. Childs, an interview with author.
106. Sevareid, an interview with author.
107. Reston, an interview with author.

Chapter Five: Samples of *Real Advocacy Journalism*™ Applied to Persistent Issues

1. Walter Lippmann, "Everybody's Business and Nobody's" for "Today and Tomorrow," April 10, 1941; a syndicated column in the *New York Herald Tribune*. The column can be found in the Walter Lippmann Collection, Microfilm, Reel No. 8.
2. Ibid.
3. Ibid.
4. Ibid
5. Ibid.
6. Ibid.
7. Ibid.
8. Ibid.
9. Ibid.
10. Ibid.
11. Ibid.
12. Walter Lippmann, "Law and Order," Metropolitan, (August 1915), p. 32.
13. Walter Lippmann, "The Dream of Troubled Spirit," "Today and Tomorrow," January 29, 1949, in the Walter Lippmann Collection, Microfilm, Reel No. 9.

14. Walter Lippmann, "Crucial Internal Question," "Today and Tomorrow," December 11, 1958, in the Walter Lippmann Collection Microfilm, Reel No. 10.

15. Walter Lippmann, "The Size of the Problem," "Today and Tomorrow," March 8, 1960, in the Walter Lippmann Collection, Microfilm, Reel No. 10.

16. These columns appeared respectively: May 29, 1958, July 4, 1957, July 21, 1959, February 5, 1957, and May 10, 1955, in the Walter Lippmann Collection, Microfilm, Reel No. 10.

17. Walter Lippmann, "The Coronation of a Queen," "Today and Tomorrow," June 2, 1953, in the Walter Lippmann Collection, Microfilm, Reel. No. 9.

18. Walter Lippmann, "The Bonds of Affection," "Today and Tomorrow," December 6, 1954 In the Walter Lippmann Collection, Microfilm, Reel No. 9.

19. Walter Lippmann, "The Living Past," "Today and Tomorrow," April 13, 1943, in the Walter Lippmann Collection, Microfilm, Reel No. 9.

20. Walter Lippmann, "To the First and Last Things," "Today and Tomorrow," May 25, 1940, in the Walter Lippmann Collection, Microfilm, Reel No. 8.

21. Henry Brandon Interviews Lippmann, *New York Times Magazine*, 1969.

22. The unfinished work can be found in the Lippmann Collection at Yale University, Manuscripts and Archives.

Chapter Six: What *Real Advocacy Journalism*™ Requires of the Practitioner

1. Reston in *Walter Lippmann and His Times*, p. 235.
2. Ibid.
3. Ibid.

4. Ibid.
5. This notion of public communication being primarily concerned with determining meanings of words is similar to the notion advanced by I.A. Richards in *The Meaning of Meaning*. (New York: Harcourt, Brace, Jovanovich, Inc.
6. This idea is introduced by Lippmann in *Public Opinion*, p., 104.
7. Ibid.
8. Ibid.
9. Ibid.
10. Ibid., p. 104-105.
11. Ibid., p. 105.
12. Ibid.
13. Ibid.
14. Ibid.
15. Ibid., pp. 105-106.
16. Ibid., p. 106.
17. Ibid.
18. Ibid.
19. Ibid., p. 107.
20. Ibid., p. 103.
21. Ibid.
22. Ibid.
23. Ibid.
24. Ibid., p. 104.
25. Ibid.
26. Ibid.
27. Ibid., p. 11.
28. Ibid.
29. Ibid.
30. Ibid., pp. 110-111.
31. Ibid., p. 111.

Chapter Seven: *Real Advocacy Journalism*™ in the Twenty-First Century: Rules of Engagement

1. Walter Lippmann, in *Walter Lippmann and His Times*, p. 235.
2. William L. Rivers, *The Opinion Makers*, (Boston: Beacon Press, 1965), pp. 60-61.
3. James Reston in an interview with the author.
4. Brown, p. 227.
5. The author interviewed James Reston, columnist, *New York Times*, in his office in Washington, DC, December 8, 1980, 10:00 a.m.
6. James Reston in an interview with the author.
7. David Weingast, "Walter Lippmann: A Content Analysis," Public Opinion Quarterly, Vol. 14, No. 2 (Summer, 1950) p. 297. (Article is found in the Walter Lippmann Collections at Yale University, Manuscripts and Archives, Box 19, Folder 401.
8. Weingast p. 297.
9. Fisher, The Columnist, (New York: Howell, Soskin Publishers, 1944), p.3.
10. Fisher, p. 2.
11. Fisher, p. 13.
12. Richard Weiner, *Syndicated Columnists*, (New York: published by Richard Weiner, 1977), p. 45.
13. Weiner, pp. 12-13.
14. Weiner, p. 13.
15. Henry Brandon, "A Talk with Walter Lippmann at 80, about this 'Minor Dark Age,'" *New York Times Magazine*, Sept. 14, 1969. Walter Lippmann Collection, Box 18, Folder 398.

BIBLIOGRAPHY

Documents

The Walter Lippmann Papers. Manuscripts and Archives Department, Sterling Library, Yale University, New Haven; Connecticut.

The Robert O. Anthony Collection of Walter Lippmann. Manuscripts and Archives Department, Sterling Library, Yale University, New Haven, Connecticut.

Interviews

Eric Sevareid, CBS News Commentator, December 8, 1980, Washington, DC.

James Reston, Syndicated Columnist, *New York Times*, December 8, 1980, Washington, DC.

Marquis Childs, Syndicated Columnist, *St. Louis Post-Dispatch*, November 1, 1980, Washington, DC.

Elizabeth Farmer Midgley, personal assistant to Walter Lippmann from January 1961-1967, January 27, 1981. Ms. Midgley is currently the producer of CBS Weekend News.

Books

Aristotle. *Nicomachean Ethics in The Basic Works of Aristotle* by Richard Mckeon. New York: Random House, 1968.

Brown, John Mason. *Through These Men*. New York: Harper and Brothers, 1956.

Childs, Marquis, and Reston, James, ed. *Walter Lippmann and His Times*. New York: Harcourt, Brace and Co., 1959.

Childs, Marquis. *Conversations with Walter Lippmann*. Boston: Little, Brown and Co., 1965.

Fisher, Charles. *The Columnist*. New York: Howell, Soskin Publishers, 1944.

James, Williams. *Pragmatism*. New York: 1928.

   The Meaning of Truth. New York: 1909.

Krieghbaum, Hillier. *Facts in Perspective*. New Jersey: Prentice-Hall, Inc., 1956.

Lippmann, Walter. *A Preface to Politics*. New York and London: Mitchell, Kennerley, 1913.

   A Preface to Morals. New York: The Macmillan Co., 1929.

   An Inquiry Into Principles of the Good Society. Boston: Little, Brown and Co., 1937.

   Early Writings. New York: Liveright Publishing Co., 1970.

Essays in the Public Philosophy. Boston: Little, Brown and Co., 1955.

Liberty and the News. New York: The Macmillan Co., 1927.

Public Opinion. New York: The Macmillan Co., 1922.

Public Persons. New York: Liveright Publishing Corporation, 1976.

The Cold War: A Study in U.S. Foreign Policy. New York; Harper, 1947.

The Method of Freedom. New York: The Macmillan Co., 1934.

The New Imperative. New York: The Macmillan Co., 1935.

The Phantom Public. New York: Harcourt, Brace and Co., 1925.

U.S. Foreign Policy: Shield of the Republic. Boston: Little, Brown, and Co., 1943.

Luskin, John. *Lippmann, Liberty and the Press*. Alabama: University of Alabama Press, 1972.

Nevins, Allen ed. *Interpretations 1933-1935*. New York: The Macmillan Co., 1936.

Nevins, Allen and Lippmann, Walter. *A Modern Reader* New York: DC Heath and Co., 1936.

Rivers, William L. *The Opinionmakers*. Boston: Beacon Press, 1965.

Rossiter, Clinton and Lare, James. *The Essential Lippmann*. New York: Random House, 1963.

Santayana, George. *The Life of Reason*. New York: 1962.

Schapsmeier, Edward L. and Frederick H. *Walter Lippmann: Philosopher-Journalist*. Washington, DC: Public Affairs Press, 1969.

Steel, Ronald. *Walter Lippmann and the American Century*. Boston: Little, Brown and Co., 1980.

Weiner, Richard. *Syndicated Columnists*. New York: Richard Weiner Publisher, 1977.

Weingast, David. *Walter Lippmann: A Study in Personal Journalism*. New Jersey: Rutgers University Press, 1949.

Wellborn, Charles. *Twentieth Century Pilgrimage: Walter Lippmann and the Public Philosophy*. Baton Rouge: Louisiana State University Press, 1969.

Wright, Benjamin F. *Five Public Philosophies of Walter Lippmann*. Austin: University of Texas Press, 1973.

Articles

Adams, James Thurslow. "Walter Lippmann," *Saturday Review of Literature*, IX (January 7, 1933), p. 361.

Allen, Henry. "Chronicling Walter Lippmann," *The Washington Post*, (September 11, 1980), p. Dl—D13.

Brandon, Henry. "A Talk with Walter Lippmann, at 80, About This Minor Dark Age," *New York Times Magazine*, (September 14, 1969).

Childs, Marquis. "The Conscience of the Critic," *Walter Lippmann and His Times*, eds. M. Childs and James Reston. New York, 1959.

"Tribute to Walter Lippmann." *Quill*, October 1973), p. 16.

Grumbach, Doris. "The Man Who Knew Walter Lippmann," *Washingtonian Magazine*, (January 25, 1975), p. 33.

Griffith, Thomas. "Comrade of the Powerful," *Time*, (September 15, 1980), p. 86.

Kraft, Joseph. "Lippmann, Yesterday. Today and Tomorrow," *The Washington Post*, (September 11, 1980), p. A19.

Lippmann, Walter. "In Defense of Suffragettes," *Harvard Monthly*, (December 1909).

"A Policy of Segregation," *Harvard Monthly*, (January 1910).

"Harvard in Politics: A Problem in Imperceptibles," *Harvard Monthly*, (December 1909).

"The Non-Athletic Boy in College," *Red and Blue*, (November 1909).

"The Discussion of Socialism: Politics and Metro-Politics," *Harvard Illustrated*, (April 1910).

"William James," *Public Persons*, Gilbert A. Harrison, ed. New York, 1976.

"An Open Mind: William James," *Everybody's Magazine*, (December 1910).

"Everybody's Business and Nobody's," in "Today and Tomorrow" column, *New York Herald Tribune*, (April 10, 1941).

"The Nixon Affair," in "Today and Tomorrow" column, *New York Herald Tribune*, (September 25, 1952).

"Law and Order," *Metropolitan*, XLII, (August 1915), p. 32.

"The Underworld," in "Today and Tomorrow" column, *New York Herald Tribune*, (April 1, 1932).

"Lawlessness," in "Today and Tomorrow" column, *New York Herald Tribune*, (December 5, 1933).

"The Dream of Troubled Spirit" in "Today and Tomorrow," column, *New York Herald Tribune*, (January 29, 1949).

"Crucial Internal Question," in "Today and Tomorrow" column, *New York Herald Tribune*, (December 11, 1958).

"The Size of the Problem," in "Today and Tomorrow," column, *New York Herald Tribune*, (March 8, 1960).

"The Coronation of a Queen," in "Today and Tomorrow" column, *New York Herald Tribune*, (June 2, 1953).

"The Bonds of Affection," in "Today and Tomorrow," column, *New York Herald Tribune*, (December 6, 1954).

"The Living Past," In "Today and Tomorrow" column, *New York Herald Tribune*, (April 13, 1943).

"To the First and Last Things," in "Today and Tomorrow", column, *New York Herald Tribune*, (May 25, 1940).

Nevins, Allen. "Walter Lippmann," *Book of the Month Club News,* (June 1943), p. 8.

Nieman Reports. "Walter Lippmann: 1889-1974," Vol. XXVIII, No. 4, Winter, 1974, p. 2.

Peer, Elizabeth. "Walter Lippmann, 1889-1976," *Newsweek*, (December 23, 19714), pp. 1 and 40.

Reston, James. "The Mockingbird and The Taxicab," *Walter Lippmann and His Times*, Marquis Childs and James Reston, ed. New York, 1959.

Salisbury, Harrison E. "Final Tribute," *New Times*, (December 1974), p. 68.

Smith, Beverly. "A Man With a Flashlight Mind," *The American Magazine*, (September 1932), p. 91.

Time. "Lippmann: Philosopher-Journalist," (December 1974), p. 56.

Weingast, David. "To What Extent Are Newspaper Columnist Read?" Bureau of Applied Social Science Research, Columbia University, (March 1947).

"Walter Lippmann: A Content Analysis," *Public Opinion Quarterly*, Vol. 14, No.2 (Summer, 1950), p. 29.

White, William Allen. "Walter Lippmann Looks at the Political Scene," *New York Herald Tribune*. October 23, 1932).

CPSIA information can be obtained
at www.ICGtesting.com
Printed in the USA
BVHW030319120521
607041BV00009B/1716/J